Why There Is No God

Simple Responses to 20

Common Arguments for the

Existence of God

Armin Navabi

To Dad, who showed me the value of learning.

To Mom, who showed me the value of caring.

Contents

Introduction

This book is meant to provide to-the-point and easy-to-understand counterarguments to many of the popular arguments made for the existence of God. Each chapter presents a short and simple explanation of the argument, followed by a response illustrating the problems and fallacies inherent in that claim. The tools offered in this book should offer you a solid foundation for building your own inquiry about the concept of God.

Who Is This Book For?

This book is written for atheists, believers and the undecided who find the concept of God an important one to examine critically and worth discussing. This book acts as a basic introduction to the debate about God, providing a springboard for new ideas to be formed and discussed.

For the already-convinced atheist, this book can help you better articulate your point of view in discussions, giving you guidance for how the reasoning behind your disbelief in God can be discussed. As an atheist, you're bound to encounter some or all of these arguments eventually when interacting with believers; understanding these arguments and seeing how others have approached them in logical ways can help you handle the same discussions.

As a believer, you may find that you disagree with much of what is said here, and that's okay. Reading this book will allow you to see what many atheists believe and how some people may question the beliefs that you hold. If you plan to defend your faith in discussions, this book can help you understand the reasoning behind the lack of belief in your opponents. Knowing this will help you debate from a more informed position, and the atheists you talk to may appreciate the fact that you've taken time to understand and consider their arguments. Knowing and appreciating the opponent's point of view can help you start a productive discussion regarding God and religion in a more constructive way.

For people who are yet undecided on the subject of God, the arguments in this book can help provide a baseline for discussion or further research about the existence of God. By reviewing many of the common arguments for the existence of God and rebuttals to them, you will have a solid foundation to use as the base of your own analysis, research and reflection.

Understanding the Burden of Proof

One concept you'll see come up repeatedly in this book is the idea of the burden of proof. During any debate, it's the job of a person making a claim to provide support, evidence and reasoning for that claim. It simply doesn't make sense to make an unfounded claim with no evidence to back it and demand that the other person to either agree with you or disprove your unfounded statement.

To better understand how the burden of proof works, consider an example by Matt

Dillahunty from *The Atheist Experience* TV show. Imagine that you're given a jar full of beans. You have no idea how many beans are in the jar, but you know that it must be either an even or an odd number. With no supporting evidence one way or the other, however, you could not say for sure whether the jar contained an even or odd number of beans. If you were to claim that it was one or the other, you would need some supporting evidence or logical reasoning. Otherwise, your claim would simply be a random guess.

The burden of proof is a necessary part of any debate, regardless of the topic being discussed. Its utility in facilitating discussion is so well established that it's required in legal proceedings as well; the prosecution must prove beyond a reasonable doubt that the defendant is guilty.

In the case of debates about God, the burden is on the believer to offer support for her position if she wishes it to be considered seriously. In reality, the only necessary argument against believing in God is simply that there is no evidence that any gods exist. An atheist doesn't need to justify her lack of belief any further. This keeps the burden of proof on the side of the claimant where it belongs. The person making a claim has to provide the evidence for its validity. Would you believe in the claim that flying pineapples exist until proven wrong without any evidence? Probably not. You would withhold belief until there is evidence to support such a claim.

All the same, it's sometimes valuable to point out the fallacies in a claimant's argument. At the very least, this creates constructive discussion where all points are considered and examined. This can also introduce doubt, causing the other person to reconsider his or her position or consider searching for evidence before accepting a claim.

Can We Say with Certainty That There Is No God?

Atheism exists on a spectrum. Some atheists claim absolute certainty in God's nonexistence. Others simply remain unconvinced and refuse to believe in a deity without compelling evidence. However, once one has a high enough level of certainty about something, they usually treat it as certain for the sake of practicality.

After all, I cannot say with absolute certainty that my wife is *not* a professional assassin hired by the People's Republic of China to exterminate me. But I don't spend time worrying about the possibility because there is no evidence whatsoever to support it. The same is true for the existence of God, although my wife being an assassin is actually more likely; that scenario, at least, would fall within the known scientific laws without contradicting the prevailing models explaining the universe.

Is There Any Value in Debate?

Many of us grew up in religious environments and began questioning what we had been taught by family, friends or the community in general.

Finding the language to talk about those doubts is a challenge, though, and having the support of others who have covered that ground is valuable.

Even if you're not changing anyone's mind, examining different arguments can help hone your own skepticism and critical thinking skills. Furthermore, some of the people you meet may be doubtful or insecure about their religion but do not know how to express those doubts; introducing them to these arguments and counterarguments might empower them to learn more and provide a better understanding of their own doubts and questions.

Whether you're using this reference as a way to validate your own views, arm yourself for debates or simply analyze the concepts of God and religion on a critical and exploratory way, this guide will provide thorough responses to 20 common arguments for the existence of God. Each chapter will introduce the claim before deconstructing it, providing sources for further study wherever relevant.

What Do We Mean by God?

For most of this book, we'll consider a god to be a conscious, supernatural being that is responsible for creating and/or sustaining the entire world or some major attributes of the world and the rules that govern it, including some examples from the Christian and Islamic definitions of God. We'll also consider theism to be the belief in this definition of a god or gods. In Chapter 13, we'll consider some other definitions for God, including deistic and pantheistic (but more on that later). For an objective overview of more views and ideologies about God, visit <u>WhatAreGods.com</u>.

Who Are We?

This book was written by Armin Navabi, a former Muslim from Iran and the founder of Atheist Republic, a non-profit organization with upwards of a million fans and followers worldwide that is dedicated to offering a safe community for atheists around the world to share their ideas and meet like-minded individuals. Atheists are a global minority, and it's not always safe or comfortable for them to discuss their views in public.

At the very least, discussing one's atheistic views can be uncomfortable and ostracizing. In some countries, expressing such views can put someone in physical danger. By offering a safe community for atheists to share their opinions, Atheist Republic hopes to boost advocacy for those whose voices might otherwise be silenced.

Further Discussions

If you have something to add to the discussion laid out in this book or want to further debate the topic, you can reach me at <u>WhyThereIsNoGod.com</u>, where I offer online video and audio discussions on the topic of God and religion.

Chapter 1: "Science can't explain the complexity and order of life; God must have designed it to be this way."

Arguably the earliest function of religion was to explain natural phenomena that primitive man could not otherwise understand. Lightning storms and volcanoes, for example, are natural forces that were once attributed to deities. Now that scientific progress has made it clear how and why many of these things occur, a God is no longer required to explain them.

The same is true for many other natural processes, and as the scientific method manages to come up with more models with better explanatory and predictive capabilities for such phenomenon, supernatural explanations prove themselves more inadequate, to say the least. Even though there are things in the world that we don't yet understand and may never truly understand, there's no reason to simply make up an explanation. In effect, belief in God is not really an answer; it's simply a way of saying, "I don't know." Yet, the existence of deities raises more questions than it solves.

In 1802, philosopher William Paley introduced "The Teleological Argument" in his book *Natural Theology* (1). In it, he argues that the universe must have been designed by an intelligent creator because it is too complex to have arisen by chance. To illustrate this, he makes an analogy to a watch: if you're walking on the beach and find a watch, you know from its complexity that a watchmaker must have created it. It would be absurd to think that the watch could have sprung up spontaneously. By his logic, complexity implies design.

Since then, many scientists and philosophers have tackled this issue and have shown that complex systems can arise without a designer. Evolution by natural selection is one such system. We'll examine the issue of complexity without design here from a more general perspective, but you can visit EvolutionSimplyExplained.com for a short and simple video explaining how evolution works.

The mathematician John Conway created a model, the Game of Life. The game shows how complexity can arise from a few simple cells following basic mathematical rules (2). In the game, a player establishes an initial pattern of "cells," then sets them loose to multiply and die according to basic mathematical calculations.
For populated spaces:

> • If a cell has one or fewer neighbors, it will die.
> • If a cell has four or more neighbors, it will die.
> • Cells with two or three neighbors will survive.

For empty spaces:

> • Cells with three neighbors become populated.

Depending on the initial circumstances, the results of each game can vary substantially. Some create incredibly complex, symmetrical designs that constantly grow. Others move toward a point of stagnation before growth stalls entirely. In every case, the resulting design occurs entirely from the mathematical laws governing the behavior of cells, not from any conscious behavior of the person playing. The game illustrates then that any system with its own rules can operate itself and move toward increasingly complex results without outside interference. To watch a couple short videos of some of these complex objects emerging from simple laws, spreading and interacting in surprisingly beautiful designs, go to: FromBasicLaws.com

Complexity Is Not the Marker of Design

The watch analogy works precisely and only because we know that watches are not natural and do not arise on their own in nature. If design were truly responsible for everything, there would be no fundamental difference between a stone and a watch because both would have been designed by an intelligent creator. Thus, we would not be able to recognize design from non-design, and the terms would be obsolete. Design exists purely in contrast to naturally- occurring phenomena.

If Complexity Requires a Creator, Who Created God?

This is perhaps the greatest problem with the idea of complexity by design. Invoking a deity doesn't solve the problem of complexity; it introduces a new problem. If all complex things really do require an intelligent creator, then why is that creator himself not bound to the same rule? Would that complex deity not require an even more complex creator, and so on, for infinity?

The complexity of the universe is something that scientists continue to explore, and we may never have all the answers. But there's nothing wrong with that. Not knowing the answer to a question is not a valid excuse for making up a fairytale to explain it.

Sources:

1).Paley, William, and Matthew Eddy. *Natural Theology: or, Evidences of the Existence and Attributes of the Deity, Collected from the Appearances of Nature*. Oxford: Oxford University Press, 2006.

2) Gardner, Martin. "Mathematical Games – The Fantastic Combinations of John Conway's New Solitaire Game 'Life.'" *Scientific American* 223, October, 1970, 120-23.

Chapter 2: "God's existence is proven by scripture."

Many religions have certain holy books that are revered as true accounts. These are called scripture, text considered sacred and either inspired or directly dictated by a deity. Many of the adherents to these religions claim that their scriptures prove the existence of their deity. The Bible and Quran are held up by many believers as both guides for belief and historical accounts of reality. Many believers claim that their holy book of choice is uniquely perfect, thus suggesting its divine origin.

This argument presupposes its premise: the people who hold up their holy scripture as evidence are the same people who already believe its contents to be true. In doing so, it falls into the fallacy of begging the question (a form of circular reasoning), where an argument's question presupposes its answer (1). This is no different than saying, "This is true because I believe it," which hardly counts as evidence.

Documents Are Not Self-authenticating

Just because something is written in a book does not mean that it's true. This is obvious. There are millions of fictional stories throughout history and plenty of other books that claim to be factual but have been proven to be false. The existence of scripture does not automatically prove anything about the veracity of what those scriptures contain.

Additionally, the scriptures themselves are rife with contradictions. Ultimately, they are books that were written by fallible humans, and though there may be some grains of historical truth within them, there is also ample hyperbole, speculation and mythology.

Scripture Is Often Inconsistent and Inaccurate

Every holy book is full of internal errors, inconsistencies and differing accounts. This makes sense when you consider that these books were pieced together by multiple authors over a span of centuries. If scripture was a document describing historical reality, the basic facts should be consistent from one account to the next.

Some biblical errors are inconsistent with the observable laws of the universe. For example, Genesis 1:1-19 states that God created the heavens and the earth on the first day of creation; the stars, sun, moon and other planets were all created on the fourth day, a full day after the creation of seed-bearing plants. This order makes no sense, as plants require sunlight to grow, even if you ignore the scientific fact that the sun and stars existed long before the earth and flowering plants.

In the Quran, several scientific errors are also apparent. For example, the Quran suggests that the earth is flat with the sun rising and setting in particular parts of the earth (18:86). Such errors make sense when considering the scientific knowledge at the time the Quran was written, but they would not make sense if the Quran had been written by an all-knowing deity, as is believed by Muslims, who hold true the belief that the Quran is the direct and exact word of God told to Mohammed.

Other scriptural problems are internal contradictions. For example, the resurrection story — arguably the single most important event in the Bible from a Christian perspective — is told in a number of different ways. Here are just a few of the inconsistencies between those versions:

- In Matthew, Jesus was buried by Joseph of Arimathea (Matthew 27:57-60). In Acts, he was buried by a different group of people (Acts 13:27-29).

- Matthew (28:2-5) and Mark (16:5) report that the women at Christ's tomb saw one person or angel. Luke (24:4) and John (20:12) say there were two.

- Mark states that Jesus died the day after Passover meal (Mark 14 - 15). John places the event on the day before the Passover meal (John 18 - 19).

When the scripture can't even come to a consensus about a simple fact like the date of Jesus's crucifixion, it's difficult to accept the accounts as being historically accurate, much less divinely inspired.

Muslims are quick to point out the supposed perfection of their holy book, the Quran. According to many Muslims, the Quran contains foreknowledge of science that predicts modern inventions and discoveries. These claims are dubious ad hoc arguments: Modern-day believers attribute these explanations to the text after the fact. If the Quran actually contained scientific breakthroughs, many of the countless believers who had studied the Quran would have made these discoveries before the scientists. That none of these scientific predictions were revealed by interpretations of the Quran until after they'd come to light by scientists makes such claims highly dubious.

Religious Texts are Man-Made and Fallible

There's a simple explanation for the errors in the Quran and Bible: these documents were written by humans, and in many cases, were stitched together from oral traditions and transcribed decades or even centuries after the events described. Bear in mind, also, that the books of the Bible are largely anonymous. Names like Matthew, Mark, Luke and John were added after the fact by editors and scribes. The actual identity of these authors is unknown (2).

Biblical scholars estimate that the oldest books of the New Testament, Paul's letters, were written around 20 years after the date of Christ's supposed resurrection. Paul was not present for any of the events described in the gospels, and he did not know Jesus personally. The gospels themselves were written even later, between 30 and 70 years after the alleged death of Jesus (2).

Jesus's contemporaries were Aramaic-speaking, illiterate commoners. They could neither read nor write, so stories were passed around orally. Like all gossip, these oral histories are bound to have transformed over time by gaining embellishments, mixing up details and forgetting important facts. Just like any other legend, from the invasion of Troy to the tales of Paul Bunyan, these stories likely contain much more poetic license than actual history.

Sources:

1) Bennett, Bo. "Begging the Question." *Logically Fallacious: The Ultimate Collection of over 300 Logical Fallacies*. EBookIt.com, 2012.

2) Ehrman, Bart D. *Jesus, Interrupted: Revealing the Hidden Contradictions in the Bible (And Why We Don't Know About Them)*. New York: HarperOne, 2009.

Chapter 3: "Some unexplained events are miraculous, and these miracles prove the existence of God."

Before discussing miracles in detail, it helps to have a firm definition of what exactly "miracle" actually means. The Collins English Dictionary defines it as "an event that is contrary to the established laws of nature and attributed to a supernatural cause." In order for something to qualify as a miracle, it must be more than statistically unlikely; it must be physically impossible without some sort of supernatural intervention.

This definition separates "true miracles" from events that are simply statistically unlikely. These latter events are noteworthy because of their rarity, but they exist within natural laws. For example, a person surviving a disease believed to be terminal only shows that the disease may not be fully understood or that the prognosis was not accurate. Our understanding of the natural world can be modified by new knowledge without needing to throw out our understanding of the laws of the universe entirely.

An Unknown Cause Is Not the Same as Divine Intervention

As a case study of perceived miracles, let's examine the belief in thunder gods within certain cultures. Throughout history, there have been many thunder gods, spread out across multiple continents and civilizations (1). In most cases, the god created thunderstorms directly through his actions, whether this meant Zeus throwing lightning bolts or the beating of a thunderbird's wings. Today, when the scientific causes of thunder are well-known, such myths seem absurd and antiquated. At the time, though, believers likely felt that thunder was a miraculous event requiring such divine explanation.

This phenomenon of ascribing supernatural causes to mysterious events is a case of "argument from ignorance" (2). This is a fallacy where a person claims that a statement is true simply because there is no evidence to the contrary, even when there is also a total lack of supporting evidence. The argument takes the form "There is no argument against P, therefore P." In other words, "There is no explanation for this event, so God did it."

Imagine this analogy: let's say that I claim that the sun runs on trillions of AA batteries. You claim that this is ridiculous. In response, I ask you to explain where the sun gets its energy from. Perhaps you don't know the answer or assume that no one yet knows the source of sun's energy. Would it be reasonable to consider this lack of understanding to be proof of my claim?

Another problem with ascribing supernatural causes to mysterious events is that they are unfalsifiable, meaning that they can't be disproved. Unfalsifiable claims hold no merit without evidence. For example, there is no way to disprove that there is not a heat-resistant population of giant rhinos living close to Earth's core. Yet, the inability to disprove such a claim does not make it likely to be true. If a claim is unfalsifiable, the burden of proof for the claim lies on whoever is making the claim.

For any given event without an explanation, an unlimited number of unfalsifiable explanations could be offered, but none of them would necessarily be true. One person might ascribe a miracle to God while someone else claims that space aliens are responsible. Without evidence to back up their claims, these explanations are equally meaningless.

Time and again, events that may initially seem miraculous later turn out to have a reasonable explanation. For example, near-death experiences are often held up as proof of the afterlife. During such an experience, a person may feel as though she is outside of her body, looking down on it, or she may experience the feeling of traveling down a dark tunnel toward a source of light. Some people report hearing the voices of departed loved ones, with these disembodied voices sometimes urging them back away from the light, which some believe may be the afterlife.

These accounts can be compelling and, for the person experiencing them, very real. However, scientific evidence suggests a biological mechanism behind these responses, and the results can be triggered manually by doctors stimulating parts of a person's brain (3).

Just because an event's cause is not immediately apparent or understandable does not mean that it must have a supernatural origin. It might simply mean that more research should be completed to understand it or even that we may never fully understand it.

Many Events Are Inherently Meaningless

The human brain is hardwired to recognize patterns, even in random, meaningless noise. Michael Shermer calls it patternicity in his 2008 *Scientific American* article, "Patternicity: Finding Meaningful Patterns in Meaningless Noise" (4). According to Shermer, this tendency toward identifying patterns and assigning causal relationship is crucial regarding our ability to survive in nature, and it's something we've evolved to do very well. As Shermer explains in a 2010 TedTalk, "[Imagine] you are a hominid three million years ago walking on the plains of Africa, and you hear a rustle in the grass. Is it a dangerous predator, or is it just the wind? Your next decision could be the most important one of your life. Well, if you think that the rustle in the grass is a dangerous predator and it turns out it's just the wind, you've made an error in cognition...but no harm. You just move away. On the other hand, if you believe that the rustle in the grass is just the wind, and it turns out it's a dangerous predator, you're lunch. You've just won a Darwin award. You've been taken out of the gene pool." This example helps demonstrate how natural selection can favor assigning causality between events (5). In a 2008 paper in the Proceedings of the Royal Society B, "The Evolution of Superstitious and Superstition-like Behaviour," Kevin R Foster and Hanna Kokko conclude that "the inability of individuals—human or otherwise—to assign causal probabilities to all sets of events that occur around them will often force them to lump causal associations with non-causal ones. From here, the evolutionary rationale for superstition is clear: natural selection will favour strategies that make many incorrect causal associations in order to establish those that are essential for survival and reproduction" (6)

This type of learning by association is prevalent in all types of animals. In the case of humans, our ability to spot patterns is quite sophisticated. Unfortunately, the brain can also be easily tricked into seeing patterns where none exist (e.g., shapes in the clouds, faces in wood grain or voices in white noise).

We're also quick to attribute meaning to things we experience, even if the event itself is inherently meaningless. As emotional human beings who form strong personal ties to one another and may care deeply for others, we cling to falsely perceived patterns possibly as a way to make sense of both tragedy and success and to, in some way, feel like we have some kind of reliable solution in situations where we sense a lack of control (7).

All of this explains why many people are so prone to believe in miracles. It does not make those miraculous experiences true. Without hard evidence to prove both the existence and cause of miracles, such events say little about the existence of God.

Improbable Events Are Not Proof of the Supernatural

Many people turn to the supernatural when they witness a highly improbable event and consider it to be a miracle rather than looking for a natural explanation. Yet an understanding of basic properties of probability laws shows that even extremely improbable events happen all the time (8). There are many examples that show that events with very small probability are not miraculous. In fact, they're commonplace. Mathematician J.E. Littlewood suggested that each one of us should expect one-in-a-million events to happen to us about once every month. Failing to recognize this is due to us ignoring the astronomically high number of events that occur which we find insignificant. Events that we do find significant, such as winning a lottery or dreaming about your mother calling you right before waking up to her call are just a tiny fraction of many other insignificant events with the same or even lower probability of occurring, such as the chance that you had a dream of your mother calling you and also running out of milk five days after at 7:21 am. As statistician David J. Hand explains, "Lives are full of events, minor and major. With so many events to choose from, it's only to be expected that some surprises will occur, even though they are incredibly unlikely when taken by themselves."

After witnessing events with very small probabilities, we might think that the laws of nature have been broken and attempt to use supernatural explanations to make sense of observing such events. But no matter how unlikely an event is, it doesn't mean that a supernatural explanation would be more likely, especially when you consider the fact that in order for us to accept such an explanation, we have to agree that scientific models of nature that have consistently and accurately explained and predicted many natural events are completely wrong simply because we have witnessed an unlikely event. Yet close analysis of such "miracles" have never led to any proof for a supernatural explanation, and, in fact, many have proven to be cheap magic tricks, hallucinations or primitive misunderstandings of natural phenomena (9).

Sources:

1) Jordan, Michael. *Dictionary of Gods and Goddesses*. Second ed. New York: Facts on File, 2004.

2) Bennett, Bo. "Argument from Ignorance." *Logically Fallacious: The Ultimate Collection of Over 300 Logical Fallacies*. EBookIt.com, 2012.

3) Blanke, Olaf, and Sebastian Dieguez. "Leaving body and life behind: Out-of-body and near-death experience." *The neurology of consciousness: Cognitive neuroscience and neuropathology* (2009): 303-325.

4) Shermer, Michael. "Patternicity: Finding Meaningful Patterns in Meaningless Noise."

Scientific American. November 17, 2008. Accessed September 1, 2014.

5) Shermer, Michael. "The Pattern behind Self-deception." TED. February 1, 2010. Accessed September 4, 2014.

6) Foster, Kevin R., and Hanna Kokko. "The evolution of superstitious and superstition-like behaviour." *Proceedings of the Royal Society B: Biological Sciences* 276, no. 1654 (2009): 31-37.

7) Shermer, Michael. *The Believing Brain: From Ghosts and Gods to Politics and Conspiracies---How We Construct Beliefs and Reinforce Them as Truths.* St. Martin's Griffin, 2012.

8) Hand, D. J. *The Improbability Principle: Why Coincidences, Miracles, and Rare Events Happen Every Day.* Scientific American, 2014.

9) Nickell, Joe. *Looking for a Miracle: Weeping Icons, Relics, Stigmata, Visions & Healing Cures.* Buffalo, N.Y.: Prometheus Books, 1999.

Chapter 4: "Morality stems from God, and without God, we could not be good people."

Religion is frequently held up as a model of correct or moral behavior. Many holy books contain rules for how people must live in order to reach Heaven or some similar blessed afterlife, and failure to follow those rules often means eternal banishment and punishment. A person who follows these rules and is "godly" is also presumed to be a moral, upright person, whereas atheists are frequently viewed with suspicion. After all, with no god to tell you how to behave, what's to stop a person from doing whatever she wants? One poll conducted by Canadian psychologists even placed atheists as more untrustworthy than rapists in the United States and Canada, showing that atheists are among the least trusted people even in North America (1).

In reality, there's no evidence that atheists as a group are any more untrustworthy or immoral than any other group. There are dishonest atheists just as there are dishonest Christians and Muslims, and there are atheists who are paragons of good behavior just like any upstanding religious person.

Indeed, religions do seem to incite violence (2) (3). This does not always imply a direct causal relationship between religion and violence, yet, this is the opposite of what you'd expect if morality really did stem from God.

Morals Change and Fall Out of Fashion

Religious texts are generally ancient, and they reflect the values of the times when they were written. Over time, our views of what is acceptable shift as our cultures progress, which makes many things found in the Bible or Quran seem outdated and highly problematic.

Consider, for example, the issue of slavery. Although there are some people who still believe that slavery is moral, the vast majority of modern Christians are unlikely to admit support for the ownership of another person. Nevertheless, the Bible has many references to slavery, carefully detailing the rules for proper slave ownership.

For example, in the Old Testament, Leviticus 25:44-46 explains that you can take slaves from neighboring nations but not enslave your own people: "Your male and female slaves are to come from the nations around you; from them you may buy slaves." Exodus 21:20-21 helpfully clarifies that a slave-owner will be punished if he strikes a slave but only if the slave dies within a few days of the punishment: "they are not to be punished if the slave recovers after a day or two, since the slave is their property."

Slavery isn't the only questionable practice condoned in the Bible. The death penalty was also wielded quite liberally in biblical times, and death was a popular punishment for sins in the Old Testament, including violations such as adultery (Leviticus 20:10), homosexuality (Leviticus 20:13), lying about virginity (Deuteronomy 22:13-21), breaking the Sabbath (Exodus 31:14-15), cursing your parents (Exodus 21:17) and more.

In Islamic teaching, it's made quite clear that anyone who turns away from the Islam should be put to death. Within some of the most trusted and authoritative Hadith collections in Islam, which is the main source of Islamic laws and ethics, Prophet Muhammad is quoted as calling for the death penalty against apostates:

> The Prophet said, "The blood of a Muslim who confesses that none has the right to be worshipped but Allah and that I am His Apostle, cannot be shed except in three cases: In Qisas for murder, a married person who commits illegal sexual intercourse and the one who reverts from Islam (apostate) and leaves the Muslims." (Sahih al-Bukhari, Vol. 9, Book 83, Hadith 17)

The Quran also advocates beating wives when they misbehave:

> "Men are in charge of women by [right of] what Allah has given one over the other and what they spend [for maintenance] from their wealth. So righteous women are devoutly obedient, guarding in [the husband's] absence what Allah would have them guard. But those [wives] from whom you fear arrogance - [first] advise them; [then if they persist], forsake them in bed; and [finally], strike them. But if they obey

you [once more], seek no means against them. Indeed, Allah is ever Exalted and Grand." (Quran 4:34)

Of course, many religious people are quick to jump to the defense of their given holy book by insisting that passages like those mentioned above are taken out of context. The claim is that critics of religion ignore the verses that come before and after and by doing so, the verses seem to mean something that they are not intended to mean. Yet many critics have actually taken the time to study these verses within their context and with a great deal of detailed analysis. It is recommended that you do not use any of these verses in an argument before studying the context in which they were mentioned in. Curiously, many believers do not demand more context when mentioning verses describing love, charity or any other positive aspect of their scripture; verses are only viewed as being out of context when the content is unflattering for believers. This sort of cherry picking is a convenient viewpoint to hold but certainly not a defensible one.

While the punishments and habits described above may have fit into the accepted morals of the authors' time and cultures, that doesn't make those cultural practices acceptable today. Today, a man who kills his wife for lying about her virginity would be persecuted as a murderer, not lauded for his moral behavior. If morality truly stemmed from an all-powerful deity, it would not change over time.

The Euthyphro Dilemma

Are things moral simply because God says so? Or does God give certain orders because they are inherently moral? This is the question at the core of Plato's Euthyphro dilemma, a problem that lies at the heart of religious debates about the divinity of moral authority (4). If morality exists separate from God's will, there is no reason to rely on God for moral behavior; one could have moral standards independently without divine feedback. On the other hand, if God creates morality simply by saying whether something is right or wrong, then that's not really morality; it's arbitrariness. Morality would become nothing more than the whimsy of a divine being blindly followed by humans.

God is Either Impotent, Evil or Non-existent

Most religions claim an all-powerful, all-loving benevolent deity. However, physical reality often contradicts this claim. Terrible things happen to people every day. Children die tragically young, natural disasters wipe out whole communities and people die from accidents and disease. These do not suggest a righteous and compassionate god. These suggest that God is either powerless, cruel or non-existent.

Worse still is the concept of hell, where non-believers suffer in eternal torment simply for disbelieving in God. Indeed, this torture is supposedly granted even to theists who believe in the wrong gods. If the Christian religion is the "right" one, every Muslim, Hindu, Buddhist and Jew would burn in hell for eternity (John 3:18-36, 2 Thessalonians 1:6-10 and Revelation 21:8), and this rule is the same for other religions that believe in the concept of hell, such as Islam:

> And whoever desires other than Islam as religion - never will it be accepted from him, and he, in the Hereafter, will be among the losers. (Quran 3:85)

> Lo! Those who disbelieve Our revelations, We shall expose them to the Fire. As often as their skins are consumed We shall exchange them for fresh skins that they may taste the torment. (Quran 4:56)

> They surely disbelieve who say: Lo! Allah is the Messiah, son of Mary...for him Allah hath forbidden paradise. His abode is the Fire... They surely disbelieve who say: Lo! Allah is the third of three; when there is no Allah save the One Allah. If they desist not from so saying a painful doom will fall on those of them who disbelieve. (Quran 5:72-73)

> For them is drink of boiling water and a painful doom, because they disbelieved. (Quran 6:70)

> And the dwellers of the Fire cry out unto the dwellers of the Garden: Pour on us some

water or some wherewith Allah hath provided you. They say: Lo! Allah hath forbidden both to disbelievers (in His guidance). (Quran 7:50)

If thou couldst see how the angels receive those who disbelieve, smiting faces and their backs and (saying): Taste the punishment of burning! (Quran 8:50)

We shall assemble them on the Day of Resurrection on their faces, blind, dumb and deaf; their habitation will be hell; whenever it abateth, We increase the flame for them. That is their reward because they disbelieved Our revelations. (Quran 17:97-98)

Lo! We have prepared for disbelievers Fire. Its tent encloseth them. If they ask for showers, they will be showered with water like to molten lead which burneth the faces. Calamitous the drink and ill the resting-place! (Quran 18:29)

But as for those who disbelieve, garments of fire will be cut out for them; boiling fluid will be poured down on their heads, Whereby that which is in their bellies, and their skins too, will be melted; And for them are hooked rods of iron. Whenever, in their anguish, they would go forth from thence they are driven back therein and (it is said unto them): Taste the doom of burning. (Quran 22:19-22)

And those in the Fire say unto the guards of hell: Entreat your Lord that He relieve us of a day of the torment. They say: Came not your messengers unto you with clear proofs? They say: Yea, verily. They say: Then do ye pray, although the prayer of disbelievers is in vain. (Quran 40:49-50)

An all-loving god would surely not damn his children to an eternity of torture simply for being born into a culture that believes in the wrong deity, follows the wrong holy book or attends the wrong type of church services.

In a debate about morality and the Christian religion, Sam Harris points out the double standard in the idea of an all-benevolent god (5). When something good happens to a believer, believers often attribute that to God. When a disaster occurs, believers often explain that God's will is mysterious and cannot be comprehended by mortals. These two claims are in opposition; if God's will cannot be comprehended, how do we know that he has good intentions at all? It certainly does not lay a solid foundation for the claim of God as the ultimate source of morality.

A Natural Explanation for Morality

As science explores the nuances of human relationships, it becomes clear that morality can exist outside of religion. In fact, it's not even limited to humans. Altruistic behaviors have been observed in animals, particularly those with complex social structures (6).

Our brains have evolved with behavioral strategies that help the survival of our genes. This is responsible for selfish desires that have helped the survival of our species, but it has also lead to altruistic desires, such as sympathy or the desire for fairness. Such natural desires have improved the survival of our genes by increasing cooperation among individuals (7).

Social animals, including humans, behave in certain ways toward others because their brains have evolved to help to ensure not only their own survival, but also the survival of their genetic kin. To make us behave in such a way, our brains create feelings, such as sympathy and desire for fairness, that are hardwired in our brains (7). As Samir Okasha of the Department of Philosophy at the University of Bristol explains: "Contrary to what is often thought, an evolutionary approach to human behavior does not imply that humans are likely to be motivated by self-interest alone. One strategy by which 'selfish genes' may increase their future representation is by causing humans to be non-selfish, in the psychological sense" (6).

Our genes are not conscious. They did not have the foresight to optimize our desires for maximizing human flourishing in modern societies; hence, fully relying on our altruistic desires is not ideal. But humans are capable of conscious foresight and thus are able to design a more comprehensive set of standards.

Ultimately, moral standards, as we understand them, are social constructs. They are tied intimately to cultural circumstances and can change over time. Nevertheless, the source of these standards is rooted in sentiments such as sympathy towards our fellow conscious beings and a desire for living in a peaceful and cooperative society. Social constructs that are based upon such desires are, at their best, designed for maximizing human flourishing while utilizing our evolutionary desires to encourage them. Given that these desires are intimately tied to our brain states, maximizing the level of happiness for the most number of people can be best achieved by a scientific understanding of how our brains function and understanding what set of standards can best encourage more human interactions that lead to a functional society (8).

Sources:

1) Gervais, Will M., Azim F. Shariff, and Ara Norenzayan. "Do You Believe in Atheists? Distrust Is Central to Anti-Atheist Prejudice." *Journal of Personality and Social Psychology* 101, no. 6 (2011): 1189-206.

2) Ellens, J. Harold. *The Destructive Power of Religion: Violence in Judaism, Christianity, and Islam*. Westport, Conn.: Praeger, 2003.

3) Hall, John R. "Religion and Violence from a Sociological Perspective." *The Oxford Handbook*

of Religion and Violence, 363-374. Oxford: Oxford University Press, 2013.

4) Jowett, Benjamin. "Euthyphro by Plato." The Internet Classics Archive. Accessed September 4, 2014.

5) Harris, Sam. "Is the Foundation of Morality Natural or Supernatural? The Craig-Harris Debate." ReasonableFaith.org. April 7, 2011. Accessed September 4, 2014.

6) Okasha, Samir. "Biological Altruism." Stanford University. June 3, 2003. Accessed September 5, 2014.

7) Dawkins, Richard. *The Selfish Gene*. 2nd ed. Oxford: Oxford University Press, 1990.

8) Harris, Sam. *The Moral Landscape: How Science Can Determine Human Values*. New York: Free Press, 2010.

Chapter 5: "Belief in God would not be so widespread if God didn't exist."

Religion has undoubtedly played a major role in the history of the world. Religious people make up the majority of the world's population, and the cultures of the world have been heavily shaped by religion throughout the centuries (1). It's easy to assume that beliefs that are so widespread must have at least some kernel of truth. After all, how could so many people believe in God if it weren't true?

In reality, there are many problems with this line of reasoning. First, it ignores the historical and cultural context in which religion formed and changed throughout the centuries. The world's cultures did not independently arrive at religious beliefs and stick with those beliefs, unchanged. Instead, religions were frequently formed through complicated circumstances, including invasions and militaristic takeovers, and ideas were stolen, borrowed, and modified by conquering nations (2).

Ultimately, the idea that a large group of people believing in something automatically makes it true is a logical fallacy called argumentum ad populum (3). Widespread belief in something does not make it real, and things can exist in reality regardless of whether you believe in them. Simply stated, the truth is true even if no one believes it, and untrue claims are still untrue even if everyone believes them.

Beliefs Do Not Influence Physical Reality

Throughout history, popular beliefs have been proven wrong repeatedly as new evidence comes to light. One widely held belief throughout history was geocentrism, or the idea that the earth was the center of the universe. This was successfully proven false in the 1600s by scientists Galileo, Copernicus, and Kepler, and today, our space program makes it clear that planets orbit suns not just in this galaxy, but all of them (4). Nevertheless, some people today continue to believe in geocentrism regardless of the ample evidence against it. A Google search on the topic turns up groups with names like "GalileoWasWrong.com" and "FixedEarth.com" that insist that centuries of scientific evidence are false. Of course, their beliefs have no effect on reality. Regardless of what these people believe, the earth continues to rotate around the sun as it always has.

Science fiction author Philip K. Dick once stated, "Reality is that which, when you stop believing in it, doesn't go away." This touches on the heart of the argumentum ad populum fallacy. Physical reality does not require belief to sustain it, and belief will not modify the rules of the universe.

Religious Belief Is Widespread, but Specific Beliefs Are Not Universal

Even if the widespread nature of religion gave significance to the claims of theists, it would be difficult to determine exactly which claims it supports. After all, the world is made up of many different religions, and none of them agree about the nature of God. If God were truly responsible for religions being so widespread, wouldn't it make sense for those religions to have more in common?

Most religions claim that theirs is the only true religion. Ultimately, if religion is meant to describe something that exists in physical reality, rather than a subjective mental or emotional truth, every conflicting religion cannot be correct and it is possible that all of them are wrong.

If anything, the pervasiveness of religion throughout history and across the world might say more about people than it does about any hypothetical deity. Similar to the evolutionary process of living beings, it is possible that religions have evolved as a self-replicating set of ideas in a way that take advantage of our natural sentiments and desires to increase the rate at which they spread while disguising their true nature (5). As the philosopher Daniel Dennett explains: "If (some) religions are culturally evolved parasites, we can expect them to be insidiously well designed to conceal their true nature from their hosts, since this is an adaptation that would further their own spread." The religions that we have today are a small fraction of all religions that have existed throughout human history. The ones that we are left with have survived because they have more effectively adapted to attract and hold the allegiance of many people.

Researchers at Ohio State University have identified 16 separate psychological desires that motivate people to seek religion, such as honor, idealism, acceptance, interdependence and fear of death (6). It is likely that religious beliefs have been so widespread because they tap into the psychological desires of many people, not because there is any external proof of their veracity.

Sources:

1) "The Global Religious Landscape." Pew Research Centers Religion Public Life Project. December 18, 2012. Accessed September 9, 2014.

2) Armstrong, Karen. *A History of God: The 4,000-Year Quest of Judaism, Christianity and Islam*. Ballantine, 1994.

3) Bennett, Bo. "Appeal to Popularity." *Logically Fallacious: The Ultimate Collection of over 300 Logical Fallacies*. EBookIt.com, 2012.

4) Hawking, Stephen. *On the Shoulders of Giants*. Philadelphia: Running Press, 2003.

5) Dennett, Daniel C. *Breaking the Spell: Religion as a Natural Phenomenon*. New York: Viking, 2006.

6) Reiss, Steven. "The Sixteen Strivings for God." *Zygon* 39, no. 2 (2004): 303-20. Accessed September 9, 2014.

Chapter 6: "God answers prayers; therefore, he must be real."

Prayer is an integral part of most religions. The idea that you can communicate your wishes, hopes and fears to an all-powerful god and receive a response is powerfully appealing. Prayer feels empowering. If you can change your world through prayer, then you are transformed from a helpless victim of circumstance into an active participant in your life. However, if prayer did not actually work, this empowerment would be nothing more than an illusion or placebo effect. Worse, this illusion could be actively harmful if it were to prevent a person from taking a different action that might actually have a proven effect on a given situation.

Proving the efficacy of prayer is actually a fairly straightforward task. To establish a cause-and-effect relationship, you could create an experiment to isolate prayer as a variable and chart whether prayer had any positive effect on the outcome of a situation. As it turns out, scientists have done precisely this.

A study of heart patients in 6 separate hospitals sought to determine whether prayers from strangers would have any effect on a person's recovery (1). After carefully following the recovery of 1,800 heart surgery patients for 30 days after the surgery, researchers found absolutely no link between prayer and recovery. However, there was a significant difference between those who were aware of the fact that they were being prayed for and those who did not know. Those who knew ended up suffering more complications, possibly due to the additional stress it caused. Being told that a high number of people are praying for your recovery might increase how severe you would perceive your illness to be and thus negatively affect your recovery. To date, there have been no reputable scientific studies showing any clear link between prayer and healing.

Confirmation Bias

Of course, despite the lack of scientific evidence to support the efficacy of prayer, many people continue to insist that prayer has affected their own lives. These claims are difficult to refute because they rely on anecdotal evidence. Anecdotal evidence is basically any claim that says, "This is true because it happened to me or someone I know." While it may be true that the event occurred, anecdotal evidence does nothing to explain why or how it happened, which is why anecdotal evidence is of little use in science.

In any case where a person claims the healing power of prayer, it's important to look at all other possible explanations. If you have a headache, you might take an aspirin and pray for it to go away. When the headache clears, how can you know which actions, if any, were responsible? You would need to study the effects of one without the other to know the effect of each. One would also need to study these effects across a wide sample size to ensure that enough data is collected and the same effect occurs every time.

When considering the case of prayer's efficacy, you would need to avoid confirmation bias. Confirmation bias occurs when you record and remember events that confirm with your views and ignore or rationalize the times it didn't (2). By seeking out evidence that supports your beliefs and ignoring or downplaying evidence that might disprove views that you already agree with, you present a skewed image of reality.

The Self Contradictory Nature of Prayer

When considering the supposed power of prayer, it's important to look at the big picture. Every day, people die, divorce, become disabled, lose their jobs or live in poverty. It's reasonable to assume that many of these people are praying for better circumstances without receiving any divine assistance.

Similarly, consider that many prayers are inherently selfish. While you pray for your niece to get a much-needed heart transplant, someone else is praying for his organ-donor son's life to be spared. Whether you're praying to win a war or a football game, you're also praying for the people on the opposing side to lose. To assume that God is not only personally invested in the minutiae of your life but that your problems are ultimately more important than other problems he may be asked to solve is both selfish and absurd considering the incredible amount of individual problems and concerns of every human on this planet.

Within religious circles, this issue becomes more insidious. Working from the assumption that God is good and hears all prayers, many believers of God offer a few possible explanations for why a prayer is not answered:

- You prayed incorrectly.
- You don't believe hard enough.
- God doesn't see fit to grant your wish.

Some of these explanations shift the blame onto a person who may already be suffering. If you had simply prayed better or been a better person, bad things wouldn't happen to you. If you're unhappy with your life, perhaps you're just too stupid to understand what's best for you. The level of potential psychological damage this could inflict on a person is huge, and this kind of emotional torment cannot be justified in the name of an unsubstantiated claim.

In order to sidestep the emotionally painful ramifications of unanswered prayers, some religious people pose the explanation in a different way. According to some believers, God answers prayers in one of three ways: "Yes," "No," and "Wait." This sounds reasonable and even wise before you realize that this explanation is inherently meaningless. In fact, those three answers cover every possible outcome of any event. Either it will happen now, it will happen later or it won't happen at all. This is true whether you pray to a deity or to a bar of soap; it does nothing to prove the existence of a deity.

The Harmful Effect of Prayer

Aside from the potential psychological damage prayer culture can inflict on those whose prayers go unanswered, prayer can be actively harmful toward people and communities. For example, parents who choose to pray for their children rather than seek medical assistance put their children at risk of serious illness or death (3). In the United States alone, about 140 children with easily treatable conditions died between 1975 and 1995 after parents withheld medical attention, relying only on prayer and faith (4). Similarly, while prayer is frequently a person's first response to a disaster, it's often the least helpful. Instead of praying for disaster victims, it would be more helpful to donate blood, send donations or volunteer. These are actions that can actually have a positive effect on someone.

Sources:

1) Dusek, Jeffery A., Jane B. Sherwood, Charles F. Bethea, Sidney Levitsky, Peter C. Hill, Manoj K. Jain, Stephen L. Kopecky, Paul S. Mueller, Peter Lam, Herbert Benson, Patricia L. Hibberd, William Carpenter, Donald W. Clem, David Drumel, Dean Marek, and Sue Rollins. "Study of the Therapeutic Effects of Intercessory Prayer (STEP) in Cardiac Bypass Patients: A Multicenter Randomized Trial of Uncertainty and Certainty of Receiving Intercessory Prayer." *American Heart Journal* 151, no. 4 (2006): 934-42.

2) Plous, Scott. *The Psychology of Judgment and Decision Making*. McGraw-Hill, 1993.

3) Roe, Maureen. "10 Failed Attempts To Heal Children With Faith - Listverse." Listverse. July 30, 2013. Accessed September 14, 2014.

4) Swan, Rita. "Letting Children Die for the Faith." *Free Inquiry*, December 31, 1998.

Chapter 7: "I feel a personal relationship with God, so I know that he is real."

Religion is highly personal for some believers, and it can be pervasive in every aspect of their lives. Cultural norms are heavily influenced by religious beliefs and practices, and many religions place a heavy focus on a person's individual relationship with a deity. Even people who are not otherwise affiliated with organized religions may feel strongly about their personal relationship with God.

The problem with using these personal relationships as proof of God's existence is that they are inherently subjective experiences. A person's experience and the emotions it causes can be genuine without the cause of that experience being based on anything outside of his or her mind. For example, we discussed near-death experiences in Chapter 3. The experience of being disconnected from your body or moving down a tunnel toward a bright light is common and feels very real for the person experiencing it. However, studies have shown that near-death experiences are caused by chemical reactions within the brain (1). The same can be true for many religious experiences.

The Temporal Lobe and Religious Experiences

When some people talk about their personal relationship with God, it's in fairly nebulous or metaphorical terms. They might discuss the way that praying makes them feel more peaceful or how reading certain passages of their preferred holy book sends chills down their spine. Others, though, use this description much more literally. Some people report having visions, hearing the voice of God or otherwise having a sensory experience.

Of course, emotional effects of prayer do not necessarily have to have a supernatural origin, and religious people are not the only ones that can have seemingly paranormal sensory experiences, and these experiences can occur in obviously secular situations. For example, mental illness and drug use can disrupt normal sensory experiences. In fact, certain hallucinogenic substances have been used in religious ceremonies for centuries among certain cultures (2).

Recent scientific discoveries have helped to explain some of the chemical reactions behind religious experiences. Part of this research began by examining people with temporal lobe epilepsy, a neurological condition which can frequently trigger religious hallucinations in addition to seizures and sensory disruptions (3). The basic conclusion we can draw here is that, although someone may have an extraordinary feeling or experience, the cause of that experience is not necessarily supernatural. As we know, the same types of experiences and feelings can be brought on by entirely natural and explainable causes.

Seeing What You Want to See

As discussed in Chapter Three, the human brain is hard-wired to spot patterns, even in random noise (4). This patternicity, as science historian Michael Shermer calls it, plays a heavy role in how religious experiences occur. People who are raised within a religious culture will generally have experiences that mirror the expectations of that culture. This means that an unexplained sensory experience might be attributed by a religious person to be a message from God. The same experience felt by another person might be variously attributed as a ghost, a demon, telepathy, alien abduction or hallucination depending on that person's individual experiences and expectations.

This creates a feedback loop, where people see what they want to believe, which then supports the beliefs they already hold. While all of this can be powerfully persuasive for the person experiencing it, none of it constitutes evidence of a deity.

The Burden of Proof

Science is uncovering a better understanding of the neurological basis behind many religious experiences (5). At the same time, science cannot nor is it expected to disprove claims based on every subjective experience a person may have. The burden of proof is always on the person making a claim, not on the person that the claim is being made to. So in order for an individual's personal relationship with God to act as proof of

God's existence, it's up to the person making this claim to substantiate it.

Imagine, for example, that a person claims that an angel came down from heaven for a visit at their home to share a cup of tea and plate of biscuits. This is a far-fetched claim, and before you believe it, you'd likely want some proof: Did anyone see the angel? Did it leave behind any evidence of its presence? Without evidence, an explanation fitting the known laws of the universe makes more sense: Either the person is lying or he is delusional or mistaken about what happened.

Assume that two different people make such a claim. One hallucinated the entire experience, while the other was actually visited by an angel. Without any evidence, the two experiences are indistinguishable from the perspective of an outsider. We have no reason to believe this claim or any other third-party account of personal experience.

A person's experiences are personal and ultimately unfalsifiable. We cannot see other people's dreams or hear the voices inside their heads. If a person makes the claim that her personal experiences reflect physical reality, she needs to be prepared to back up those claims with actual evidence. Subjective experiences and anecdotal evidence are not sufficient to provide proof of a deity's existence, and wanting to believe something does not make it true.

Sources:

1) Blanke, Olaf, and Sebastian Dieguez. "Leaving body and life behind: Out-of-body and near-death experience." *The neurology of consciousness: Cognitive neuroscience and neuropathology* (2009): 303-325.

2) Pinchbeck, Daniel. *Breaking Open the Head: A Psychedelic Journey into the Heart of Contemporary Shamanism*. New York: Broadway Books, 2002.

3) Ramachandran, V. S., Sandra Blakeslee, and Oliver Sacks. *Phantoms in the Brain: Probing the Mysteries of the Human Mind*. New York: William Morrow, 1999.

4) Shermer, Michael. *The Believing Brain: From Ghosts and Gods to Politics and Conspiracies---How We Construct Beliefs and Reinforce Them as Truths*. St. Martin's Griffin, 2012.

5) Beauregard, Mario, and Vincent Paquette. "Neural Correlates Of A Mystical Experience In Carmelite Nuns." *Neuroscience Letters* 405 (2006): 186-90.

Chapter 8: "It's safer to believe in God than be wrong and go to Hell."

In the mid-1600s, mathematician and philosopher Blaise Pascal introduced an argument that could come to be called Pascal's Wager. His argument discusses the issue of religious belief from a mathematical standpoint, determining that the cost of belief is lower than the cost of atheism. The wager takes the following format:

> • If you believe in God and he does exist, you will be rewarded with eternity in Heaven.
> • If you believe in God and he does not exist, nothing will happen to you.
> • If you reject belief in God and he does exist, you will be doomed to an eternity in Hell.
> • If you don't believe in God and he doesn't exist, nothing will happen to you.

Based on these suppositions, Pascal reasons that it's always safer to live as though God is real because if there is a god and you believe in him, the benefits are infinite. If you believe in God and turn out to be wrong, you will have lost nothing; if you don't believe in God and turn out to be wrong, the consequences are dire (1).

Pascal was an admittedly brilliant mathematician, and his contributions to mathematics are valuable. As a theological argument, however, Pascal's Wager breaks down for several important reasons. First, it's important to realize that the wager does nothing to prove the nature of God. It's not an argument for the existence of god at all, actually; it's an argument against atheism based on the relative opportunity versus cost of belief.

Second, you must recognize the limitations of Pascal's premise. As a Christian apologist, his argument works only for the Christian God. It ignores the possibility of any other deity and assumes that the motives of God are consistent with the teachings of basic Christian theology. Viewed in the context of world religions, the wager falls apart completely. The wager is based on the mathematic analysis of four outcomes. However, if you throw the multitude of world religions into the equation, the premises and mathematic analysis becomes much more complex and convoluted, making your chances of a successful wager significantly slimmer.

Choosing the Right God

Multiple religions exist throughout the world, and the messages of most are at odds with each other. Among the two largest religions (Christianity and Islam), it's clear that worshiping the right deity in the appropriate way is crucial to finding salvation. To enter Heaven as a Christian, you must be "saved" by believing in Jesus as your savior (The Bible: John 3:18-36, 2 Thessalonians 1:6-10 and Revelation 21:8). According to some verses in the Quran, non-Muslims will end up in Hell (The Quran 3:85, 4:56, 5:72-73, 7:50, 17:97-98, 98:6).

All of this means that belief in God alone is not sufficient to enter Heaven.

It also means that if you happen to believe in the wrong god, you can still end up in Hell—even if you follow the tenets of your chosen religion perfectly. For example, if the Judeo-Christian God was real and the Bible accurate, every Muslim, Buddhist, and Hindu would go to Hell, regardless of how devoutly they believed their own religion. The Bible says: "He will punish those who do not know God and do not obey the gospel of our Lord Jesus. They will be punished with everlasting destruction and shut out from the presence of the Lord and from the glory of his might" (2 Thessalonians 1:8-9). Similar verses are seen in the Quran: "And whoever desires other than Islam as religion - never will it be accepted from him, and he, in the Hereafter, will be among the losers" (3:85). According to some definitions of Islam in the Quran, this may include Jews and Christians but not members of non-Abrahamic religions and people with no religious affiliation, which together account for about 45% of the world's population. Remember, also, that not every religion supports the idea of Heaven and Hell. If the "right" god came from a religious tradition without such an afterlife, Pascal's wager ceases to work.

Pascal's wager assumes a very narrow and specific definition of God. Even if there were a god, there is simply no way to know that the assumptions laid out in the wager are actually accurate. For example, why would an all-powerful and benevolent deity banish his creations to Hell for disbelief? It's equally likely that a deity might reward his followers for being skeptical, in which case Pascal's wager crumbles.

Moreover, believing in God simply to avoid the punishment of Hell is an empty type of belief. Surely, an all-knowing god could identify this insincerity and reward only true believers, not those who worshiped just to avoid consequences.

What's the Harm?

Pascal suggests that there is nothing to lose in believing, even if God is not real. This is not necessarily true. Belief in God can come with a high price for some. Some of the most powerful nations in the world are making major political decisions based on a belief in God. Wars are fought using religion, and the rights of some individuals and groups are oppressed in the name of God. The lives of billions of people around the world are affected by religious beliefs. Blindly accepting claims and making decisions as if they were true in the hope that our chosen deity exists and will reward our efforts seems like a very poor wager when there is no evidence to support that choice and especially if real people are suffering as a result.

Sources:

1) Popkin, Richard H. The Columbia History of Western Philosophy. New York: Columbia University Press, 1998.

Chapter 9: "God isn't defined. God cannot be comprehended or described. One must simply have faith."

When other arguments fail, many theists turn toward an appeal to faith. This argument takes several forms:

- "I don't need evidence; I just have faith."
- "If you had faith, you'd know that it was true."
- "God cannot be comprehended or understood. You just have to believe."

In every case, the appeal to faith is ultimately fallacious (1). By this definition, an appeal to faith is also an abandonment of reason; when one has no logical argument for a claim, they turn to faith as an explanation for their belief. Stating that you have faith in something might explain why you believe in it, but it does nothing to compel anyone else to believe the same way. The mere fact that one has faith in a belief system cannot possibly be considered reason enough for another to adopt that belief system as well.

The Absurdity of Faith as an Argument

Faith is often invoked in an argument when the person making a claim runs out of rational explanations to support his beliefs. It's a distraction from the fact that there is no real evidence. Once faith enters the equation, the argument can quickly dissolve into absurdity, as absolutely any claim could be "supported" by faith.

You might believe that your dog is secretly a werewolf, that you are abducted by aliens every night while you sleep, or that the president is actually a holographic illusion. You have no proof to substantiate these claims, but you have faith that you're correct. That doesn't mean anyone would be compelled to believe you, however; if anything, the strength of your conviction might be viewed more as a sign of insanity than the truth of the claim. If you make a claim, you must be prepared to back it up with evidence.

Some people might try to defend their argument from faith by saying something like, "Don't you have faith that the sun will rise tomorrow?" But this is not analogous. We can know with a high degree of certainty that the sun will rise because we know the natural processes that govern the movement of the earth in our solar system. From observable evidence, we know that the world works in a certain way. We don't need faith; we have evidence. The same cannot be said for a claim that has no evidence.

God Cannot Be Defined

Some theists do not come out and make an appeal to faith directly. Instead, they'll say things like "God cannot be described" or "God cannot be comprehended by the human mind." Regardless of the form these claims take, they always come down to an appeal to faith. If you cannot comprehend or describe something, you can't possibly have a rational justification for believing in it. An indescribable god may be unfalsifiable, but it is also unprovable. For example, if I were to present an archaeological research paper regarding a completely new type of pottery that had never been seen before and was previously unknown of, my colleagues would expect me to accurately describe this pottery in order to clarify its typography and confirm its existence. If I claimed not to know what it even looked like, any explanation would not make sense in the context of my claim that this pottery exists. If the pottery existed, in order to make the claim of it being a reality, I should at least be able to clarify its defining characteristics, such as color, glaze, decoration, thickness, form, etc. It simply wouldn't make sense for me to claim such a pottery exists yet not even be able to clarify whether it was brown or not. If I don't know or could not discover its characteristics, then I also can't know if it exists.

People faced with the idea of a god who cannot be described or comprehended may feel that there is insufficient evidence to say confidently that the deity does not exist. They do not, however, have any reason to believe that it does, and barring evidence in favor of a deity, they will continue living their lives as though there were no God.

The Irrelevance of Faith

As discussed in Chapter 5, believing in something does not make it true. Reality exists independently of your beliefs. It's possible to believe in things that are false, and reality continues to be true even if you don't believe in it.

For example, say you are given a wrapped package. You believe that the package contains a diamond necklace. However, in reality, the package contains a *Game of Thrones* DVD box set. No matter how firmly you believe in the diamond necklace, that does not change the actual contents of the package. Your faith in the necklace does not affect the nature of what is actually inside of the box.

When faced with any given situation or decision, there are many more ways to be wrong than to be right. With the hypothetical wrapped box, for example, you could guess dozens or thousands of times what might be inside, and all of those guesses might be wrong. If you have no evidence to support your claim, there is no reason to assume that your guess is correct, and there is certainly no reason why anyone else should believe that your guess is the right one.

Sources:

1) Bennett, Bo. "Appeal to Faith." *Logically Fallacious: The Ultimate Collection of over 300 Logical Fallacies.* EBookIt.com, 2012.

Chapter 10: "There's no evidence that God doesn't exist."

When confronted with criticism, some theists will pull out this argument in an attempt to shift the burden of proof toward the critic. Although this tactic can feel very clever, it opens a door to absurdity. This argument seems to suggest that we believe in everything, even things we have yet to think about, until that belief is proven false. That's simply not a logical way to perceive reality.

If the criteria for something being accepted as true was based purely on there being no evidence against it, an endless number of hypothetical objects could suddenly become "real." This has been the source of numerous playful thought experiments by skeptics around the world:

• The flying spaghetti monster, who created the earth with his noodly appendage (1).
• The invisible pink unicorn, whose "believers" logically know that she must be invisible because she has not been seen, yet have faith that she's pink (2).
• The dragon in Carl Sagan's garage, a thought experiment he describes in *The Demon-Haunted World*. The dragon is invisible, floats in the air, generates no heat and is incorporeal, thus evading all forms of sensory detection (3).
• Russell's Teapot, a hypothetical teapot that you cannot prove isn't orbiting the sun (4).

Of course, all of these examples were designed in good fun. Bertrand Russell does not actually believe that there is a teapot orbiting the sun. However, there is no way to definitively prove that these fanciful claims *aren't* true, which demonstrates the total absurdity of this line of thinking.

Ad Hoc Arguments

Carl Sagan's invisible dragon argument shows the futility of ad hoc arguments in explaining reality. An ad hoc argument is one that makes excuses to rationalize away the valid criticisms of an argument without any evidence to support it (5). When the claimant desperately wants something to be true, she'll often employ an ad hoc argument to counter any arguments to her claim.

The dragon in Carl Sagan's hypothetical garage cannot be seen because it's invisible. A skeptic might press for evidence. But its footprints cannot be observed because it hovers in the air, and the dragon's invisible fire is heatless. A rationalization can be formed to explain the absence of any form of evidence. These rationalizations don't make the original claim true. Indeed, it's easiest to make ad hoc arguments about things that don't really exist because that frees you up to create increasingly fanciful arguments.

When applied to theism, this ad hoc reasoning can be seen in the increasingly vague descriptions of God. The rationalizations discussed in the last chapter – that God cannot be comprehended or described – fall under the ad hoc fallacy. Such rationalizations make God so vague that it becomes impossible to refute the idea, but they get the claimant nowhere closer to proving his claim.

Disbelief Is Not the Same as Belief in Something Else

Telling an atheist to prove that there is no God automatically assumes that this is what the atheist believes. While gnostic atheists confidently believe that there are no deities, many other atheists are agnostic atheists. In other words, these people do not believe in any gods, but they do not claim to be certain that any gods do not exist. Gnostic atheists, meanwhile, do feel confident saying that no gods exist. Both are valid types of atheism. It is important to note that atheism and agnosticism are not mutually exclusive. To understand the difference between atheism and agnosticism, visit AtheismVsAgnosticism.com.

Lack of belief in deities is enough to classify someone as an atheist. Lacking belief in something does not mean that you believe it to be false; it just means that you have no conviction that it's true. For example, a friend of yours may believe that Ford is the best car company in the world. You have no particular opinion in the matter one way or the other. You don't believe that Ford is better than any other car brand, but you also don't know that it's not the best car brand. In this situation, you would be agnostic about your friend's claim.

In actuality, most people are atheist about at least some gods. After all, there are thousands of gods throughout the history of world theology, but the majority of religious people have no problem in disbelieving Zeus, Thor or Anubis (6). Jews and Muslims have no trouble denying the divinity of Christ. Monotheists are well practiced in disbelieving other gods. As Richard Dawkins put it, atheists simply take this one god further.

Religions demand perfect evidence from anyone rebutting their claims but offer none for their own claims. If faced with convincing evidence in favor of any deity, we should reconsider our position. But we need to ask questions and go where the evidence leads us, rather than try to lead the evidence where we like. By questioning everything, we follow the evidence, rather than trying to force the evidence to fit our presupposed conclusions.

Sources:

1) Henderson, Bobby. "About." Church of the Flying Spaghetti Monster. Accessed September 15, 2014.

2) Ashman, Alex. "The Invisible Pink Unicorn." H2g2. February 8, 2007. Accessed September 15, 2014.

3) Sagan, Carl, and Ann Druyan. "The Dragon in My Garage." The Demon-Haunted World: Science as a Candle in the Dark. Ballantine Books, 1997.

4) Russell, Bertrand. "Is There a God? [1952]." *In The Collected Papers of Bertrand Russell*. Vol. 11: Last Philosophical Testament. London: Routledge, 1997.

5) Bennett, Bo. "Ad Hoc Rescue." *Logically Fallacious: The Ultimate Collection of over 300 Logical Fallacies*. EBookIt.com, 2012.

6) Jordan, Michael. *Dictionary of Gods and Goddesses*. 2nd ed. New York: Facts on File, 2004.

Chapter 11: "If there is no God, where did everything come from? Without God, there is no explanation."

The origin of the universe is one of the greatest unanswered questions in the history of mankind. Humans have been debating it for thousands of years, and every religion attempts to posit a different explanation. In Chapter 1, we discussed the issue of complexity and touched on the origins of life. Questions about the origin of the universe – or, indeed, the origin of reality in general – are more challenging for science to tackle head-on. The simple answer is: we don't know. We may never know exactly how the universe was formed or what, if anything, came before it, although science does have a few ideas to explore. However, not knowing the answer does not give us free range to make something up.

It's human nature to be uncomfortable with the unknown. Historically, humans have filled these uncertain areas with a deity or other supernatural claims to explain what they have yet to discover. This creates a "god of the gaps," wherein God is invoked as an explanation in events that humans don't yet understand. The problem with this, of course, is that scientific knowledge is always expanding, and the gaps continue to grow smaller. We have identified many of the natural causes behind these gaps throughout our history and have yet to come across God in any of them. It's possible that this pattern will continue in the future, leaving little room for God as a weak explanation, and the current monotheistic ideas of God will become as outdated for future generations as the Greek pantheon is today.

The Prime Mover

The cosmological argument for God is an attempt to infer God's existence from the known facts of the universe. Essentially, this argument states that because everything is derived by cause and effect, something must have caused the universe to be created. However, although many physical laws of the universe do generally work in a cause-and-effect way, that does not necessarily mean that God is the cause.

If you follow events backwards through time, you will always find a preceding event that led to it, but theists reason that this chain of events could not go on forever. Something must have started all of it into motion. Since events cannot cause themselves, something else must have existed first to cause all of these things.

This might seem like a reasonable argument, but it falls victim to the same problem as the hypothetical God behind the argument from design, as discussed in Chapter 1: if everything has a cause or a creator, then who created God? And who, then, created the entity that created God? Rather than solving the problem of infinite causality, the cosmological argument simply recreates the problem using different terms. God is used as an answer, but in reality, the issue of God simply raises new questions. You cannot solve a mystery by using a bigger mystery as the answer.

This issue falls prey to the "special pleading" fallacy, a specific type of hypocrisy that arises when someone realizes that the solution he's offering fails to live up to the rules he's already established (1). In this type of fallacy, the rules apply to everything but the arguer's solution, which gets a special exception for the rule despite there being no clear reason why that exception should exist in the first place. If everything requires a creator, why doesn't God? And if God does not require a creator, why must everything else?

Indeed, if we can accept the idea that something could exist without being created – as theists claim for their god(s) – why could this same logic not apply to the universe itself? This would cut out the middleman and make just as much sense as a deity without the other complications that belief in God can create.

Misunderstanding Physics

Many theists who pose the cosmological argument do so from a place of misunderstanding physics. Most specifically, they will cite the First Law of Thermodynamics, stating that "matter and energy cannot be created or destroyed (2)." Note that mass is a form of energy. From this, they postulate that something cannot come out of nothing in the natural world, which necessarily means that a supernatural explanation is required.

While the theistic argument claims that the First Law of Thermodynamics proves that there needs to be a source for all matter and energy in the universe, in fact, there are other ways that this could be true. For example, the universe, or multiple universes, could have existed forever with the same amount of matter and energy. Or the universe's, or multiple universes', positive and negative energy could add up to zero. We simply don't yet know the complete workings and laws of the universe at this point in time, but that doesn't mean that we can fill in the gaps of our knowledge with God. In fact, if God can create matter and energy, why couldn't a natural process that we do not understand yet do the same as well?

Additionally, the very idea of invoking natural laws as a defense of the supernatural is inherently absurd. If a deity truly existed who could break all natural laws and exist outside of reality, there would be no need for him to conform to the laws of physics. Requiring science to support your opinion about some things, like thermodynamics, while ignoring it when it disagrees with your other beliefs, like evolution, is a flagrant misappropriation of scientific principles.

The Cosmological Argument Says Nothing about God

Even if we were to accept that the universe required some sort of "prime mover," or originating force, there is no evidence to suggest that this force must conform to any of the traits generally attributed to a god. If indeed there were a creator, there's no reason why that creator should necessarily be intelligent or have any sort of consciousness at all. There is certainly no reason why that creator should in any way resemble the god(s) described by any of the world's religions. Note that there is also no evidence to suggest that this originating force must be supernatural or spiritual in nature to begin with. After all, an originating force may just as well be an event involving physical laws.

Even if the cosmological argument were to be true in the sense of a prime mover, that claim does nothing whatsoever to prove the existence of a deity unless the definition of "deity" is confined purely to mean "forces that created the universe." If that were the case, you could just as easily call electricity, gravity or the strong nuclear force a god. The general definition of a god among religious people demands consciousness and intelligence in that god, and there is absolutely no evidence that such consciousness exists in any natural forces currently known to man.

Sources:

1) Bennett, Bo. "Special Pleading." *Logically Fallacious: The Ultimate Collection of over 300 Logical Fallacies*. EBookIt.com, 2012.

2) Atkins, Peter. *The Laws of Thermodynamics*: A Very Short Introduction. Oxford: Oxford University Press, 2010.

Chapter 12: "My religion/God has helped me so much. How could it not be real?"

For many believers, religion does more than provide answers about the nature of reality or moral life. It also provides a social framework and support system, and this can make up the backbone of a person's cultural identity. In some places, culture and religion are so tightly entwined that they become inseparable, and rejecting the tenets of religion can impose feelings of isolation.

To be sure, churches, mosques, temples and other religious communities have many beneficial features. They host social events and facilitate friendships. They provide support, offer counseling services and pool resources to offer financial support. Some religious groups are active in their communities, and many well-known charitable organizations have religious roots.

However, the benefits of religious communities do not prove the existence of a deity. If anything, what they do prove is that people can be mobilized to do great things to help themselves and each other when united under a common goal. The benefits of belonging to a religious community are not uniquely theistic, and it's possible to get similar results through a secular community without any of the more harmful aspects of religion.

There is no evidence to suggest that God helps people. There is, however, ample evidence that people can help themselves and each other. As such, the benefits of a religious community can be found in any group of people united toward a common cause. Many atheist groups and organizations also exist to provide a sense of community and support for non-religious people.

Positive Experiences Do Not Prove God

In Chapter 7, we discussed the difficulty of disproving a person's subjective experience, but we also showed how those subjective experiences could not serve as evidence to support the claim of a deity. The same is true for a person's experience as a member of a church, mosque or temple. A person's experiences within a particular religious community may be positive, but those experiences are by no means guaranteed or serve as proof of the existence of God. Atheists and theists alike can suffer from depression or overcome adversity; this does not affect the argument for God in any way.

Helpful people or beneficial communities are not localized to any particular religion. Many advocacy groups are secular, such as Doctors Without Borders and UNICEF, and it's hard to ignore the contributions these groups have made. Clearly, it's possible to make a positive impact without God; a beneficial community, therefore, does not require a deity nor provide evidence for one.

Furthermore, not everyone who attends church will have a positive experience. Additionally, many terrible crimes have been committed in the name of God, including wars, genocide and suicide cults. If the positive things that can happen in church are evidence of God's benevolence, then would these negative outcomes be evidence of God's cruelty? To suggest otherwise would be to fall into the fallacy of "special pleading," as discussed in the last chapter.

What About the People God Doesn't Save?

For every story about how God or religion has brought about good things or events in a person's life, there are also religious people suffering. Believers experience hardship. They can get sick, suffer from depression, endure domestic abuse or die prematurely, just like anyone else. If God is really responsible for all things that happen in a person's life, he must also be responsible for the bad things or at least allow them to happen.

As mentioned, religion has also been responsible for a lot of terrible things throughout history, both on an institutional and personal level. If you accept that God is responsible for the good things that happen in a person's life, without evidence, how can you not also accept that God is responsible for people murdering their families, participating in religious wars or discriminating and harming others based on religious beliefs and viewpoints (1)?

As discussed in Chapter 6, prayer culture can have an insidiously devastating effect on an individual. According to many believers in the power of prayer, all things that happen are God's will, and you can change your circumstances through an appeal to the deity. For many, this means that if their prayers are not answered, it's their own fault; they prayed incorrectly, didn't believe enough, are not godly enough or do not ask for the right thing. On the other hand, if things are going well in your life, it's because your prayers have been answered or because God is good and merciful.

This can create an environment of crippling insecurity and learned helplessness. These religious messages teach people – especially young people – that they are not in control of their own lives and do not have the power to shape their own destinies. The psychological consequences of this can become devastating. Psychologist Dr. Marlene Winell refers to such problems as Religious Trauma Syndrome, a cluster of symptoms including anxiety, depression and social functioning troubles caused or exacerbated by religious indoctrination (2).

Sources:

1) "God Told Me to Do It." Huffington Post. Accessed September 15, 2014. http://www.huffingtonpost.com/tag/god-told-me-to-do-it/.

2) Winell, Marlene. "Religious Trauma Syndrome." British Association for Behavioural & Cognitive Psychotherapies. Accessed September 16, 2014.

Chapter 13: "God is love; God is energy."

In Chapter 9, we discussed the tendency of some religious people to redefine God in such a way that their claims become unfalsifiable. A vague concept of God becomes impossible to disprove, but it is also impossible to support with any type of evidence. If you claim that God exists but cannot say exactly what God is, your claim is ultimately meaningless.

Some people attempt to define God as being synonymous with things that are already proven to exist: nature, the universe, love, energy, etc. For example, author Brendan McPhillips suggests in his article, "Einstein Proves the Existence of God," that God is the energy that creates mass as described in the famous equation $E=MC^2$ (1). According to McPhillips, the energy responsible for creating the universe and everything within it is God.

The problem with this is that we already have the word "energy," and it suits this purpose of describing energy just fine without using the word "God." God is a term that comes with a lot of additional baggage. For most theists, God does more than create the universe; he's also responsible for answering prayers, passing divine judgment or causing things to happen in an individual's life. God has a consciousness and ability to think, speak, act and make decisions.

There is no evidence whatsoever that energy has consciousness or self-awareness. Without those qualities, nothing about energy is divine or supernatural. Saying that God is energy serves only to talk about the proposed definition of words. It does little to provide more information about the physical world, and it certainly says nothing about the nature of existence of a deity.

Definitions of God

There are several types of theists, each of them defining God in their own way but all of them generally agreeing on some basic premises. Monotheists, like many Christians, Jews and Muslims, believe in a single supernatural, all-powerful deity. Polytheists, like Hindus, believe in multiple deities or a single deity who can take multiple forms, depending on the specifics of their particular belief system. In either case, when these people refer to God, they have something very specific in mind. For the three Abrahamic religions, Christianity, Islam and Judaism, God is an all-powerful, benevolent deity who is responsible for creating and maintaining order in the universe. This deity is believed to play a role in every person's day-to-day life, answering prayers, performing miracles and punishing sinners.

Some people believe in God without subscribing to a particular religion or adhering to a specific definition as laid out by a religious text. Many such people are deists who believe in an intelligent, supernatural being who created the world and established all of its natural laws. After that event, this impersonal deistic god plays no further role in the universe; he doesn't answer prayers, perform miracles or have any effect on the lives of individuals or the things that happen in the universe.

Although the deist god is quite different from the god of most theists, he is nevertheless presumed to be an intelligent, supernatural being with some sort of consciousness. Although deists often do not subscribe to any particular church or religious affiliation, they are nevertheless theists. The problem with deism is that it's ultimately impossible to prove; a passive, non-intervening god is indistinguishable from the complete absence and nonexistence of a god in our universe, as neither of these scenarios include a deity intervening or affecting our world.

For some people, "god" is simply a word used to describe certain concepts, like natural laws or the universe itself. A pantheist is a person who believes that the words "god" and "nature" are synonymous. In some cases, people with these beliefs may believe that these natural forces are inherently divine. Others may see some sort of spiritual power in nature without ascribing it to a deity. They do not believe in the existence of a supernatural sentient being that exists apart from the natural world. For these people, the usage of the word "god" is metaphorical, a poetic device used to ascribe a sense of spirituality or wonder to the natural world, not the name of any real deity. Pantheism is, as Richard Dawkins put it, "sexed up atheism" (2).

All of this quibbling about language may seem inconsequential, but it underlies an important point about the way we approach language and our world. If the word "god" can mean anything to anyone, then it essentially carries no meaning. The very concept of human language and communication depends on words and sounds that are clearly defined and have a consistent meaning throughout the population of those who use that language.

Words Are Not Objects

The words used to describe an object have no effect on the nature of the object itself. When imagined in other terms, it becomes clear how fallacious the argument "God is energy" really is:

"God" is my pet cat.
My cat exists.
Therefore, God exists.

All this serves to prove is that my cat's name is God. It does not imbue God the Cat with any of the qualities people assign to deities: omniscience, omnipotence, benevolence or having supernatural abilities. Thus, calling my cat God is meaningless in terms of defining and proving the existence of a deity. The same is true for "God is energy" or any other similar claim. Unless you are also claiming that energy has the supernatural abilities generally attributed to deities, the statement is void of meaning. Just like claims for the existence of the Abrahamic God, claiming that energy, love, gravity or any other natural force has supernatural abilities can be ignored if not supported by verifiable evidence.

We already have words for things we know to exist. We don't need to redefine those words, and doing so only serves to create confusion and a breakdown of effective communication and language understanding. The word "god" can mean anything, but it has a generally accepted definition that people have used for thousands of years. If the word is to retain any meaning at all and not become completely useless, we must continue using it in the way it has always been defined: as the description of a conscious supernatural deity who created our world or, at least, some major attributes of it and the rules that govern it.

As illustrated throughout this book, there is no evidence whatsoever that an intelligent supernatural entity exists. Saying that God is energy does not support the theist concept of a god and thus cannot act as any sort of counterargument against atheism.

Sources:

1) McPhillips, Brendan. "Einstein Proves the Existence of God!" Brendan McPhillips. Accessed September 16, 2014.

2) Dawkins, Richard. *The God Delusion*. Boston: Houghton Mifflin, 2006.

Chapter 14: "The laws of logic prove the existence of God."

One relatively new counterargument to atheism is the so-called transcendental argument for God, or TAG, as popularized by Matt Slick of Christian Apologetics & Research Ministry (CARM) (1).

Although the transcendental argument for God as displayed on the CARM website is fairly new, the ideas behind it trace back at least as far as Immanuel Kant (2). Kant introduces the idea and structure of the transcendental argument using certain logical truths or laws that are universal, unchangeable and absolute.

What the Transcendental Argument Actually Says

From a philosophical standpoint, there are three logical absolutes:

1. Law of Identity: Something is what it is and isn't what it is not. Something that exists has a specific nature. For example, an apple is that apple, and a rock is that rock. In other words, whatever is, is.

2. Law of Non-contradiction: Two opposing statements cannot both be true. For example, "this is an apple" and "this is a rock" cannot both be true if the object in both statements is referring to the same thing. In other words, nothing can both be and not be.

3. Law of Excluded Middle: A statement cannot be both true and false at the same time in the

same sense. For example, the statement "this is an apple" is either true or false; an object being an apple can't be both true and false at the same time. In other words, everything must either be or not be.

These laws are necessarily absolute. They are always true, and there can be no exceptions. Someone who says, "This rock is an apple," makes no sense, as that statement defies the laws of logic; in order for a discussion to take place, all parties involved must agree that rocks, once defined, are always rocks and adhere to their definitions.

The TAG argument builds on these laws of logic to provide the following "proof" of God:

1. Logical absolutes exist.
2. These laws of logic are conceptual in nature, not physical. They do not exist anywhere in the physical world.
3. Because these absolutes are conceptual, they must have been conceived in a mind.
4. However, these laws are perfect and absolute. Human minds are not perfect or absolute.
5. Logical absolutes are true everywhere and are not dependent on human minds.
6. Therefore, these laws of logic must exist in a perfect, absolute, transcendental mind.
7. That mind is called God.

Put in another way, logical absolutes must be the product of a mind, and these laws are absolute, so there must be an absolute mind behind them with that mind being God.

In order for a logical proof to work, two conditions must be met: The premises must be true, and the structure must support the premises to their logical conclusion. Structurally, the argument is logically sound; if every premise were true, then the outcome would also be true. However, as we shall see, the premises are not true, which invalidates the argument entirely.

The Fallacy of Equivocation

The problem with the TAG is that the laws of logic are descriptive, not prescriptive. In other words, the laws are simply a description of things we know to be true. The universe does not conform to logical absolutes because someone thought them up and is holding reality to that standard. These absolutes exist purely to describe patterns that we have observed as true in reality. To understand the difference between a descriptive and prescriptive law, consider this example:

Gravity is a descriptive law. Isaac Newton didn't create gravity. It existed before he identified it and would have continued existing regardless of whether he had ever given it a name. The laws of gravity are simply observations made by scientists that explain natural processes.

The traffic speed limit is a prescriptive law. It was created and enforced by people, and it's meaningless without such enforcement. If no one came up with a speeding limit or held people accountable for speeding, speed limits would cease to exist.

In the same way, the laws of logic are descriptive. No one made them up or wrote them in a handbook somewhere for them to exist. They were simply observed as always being true (rocks are always rocks because if a rock were anything else, it would cease to be a rock). Because the laws of logic are not prescriptive, they do not require the mind of a deity or any other mind to exist. Human minds can identify them and put them into words, but the phenomena these laws refer to would continue to exist regardless of whether a deity or anyone else thought about them.

Proponents of TAG conflate the description of logical laws with the natural phenomena they refer to. Equating an object with its description is like equating a photograph of a car with the real thing; although the photograph accurately depicts an image of the car, you cannot apply the qualities of the photo in accurately describing the real car. Otherwise, you might erroneously extrapolate that cars are flat and fit in the palm of your hand. The same is true for the laws of logic. The statement "A=A" is a conceptual description of a physical property. The statement itself requires a mind to describe it. However, the physical property would remain true, with or without a mind to conceive it.

What this means is that these descriptions themselves are what is purely conceptual. But the laws they describe are not conceptual. What these laws refer to is the consistency of existence, which exists whether or not they're being described or identified by a mind. A rock is always a rock because it exists in reality. If there were no mind to observe the rock, it would still be a rock. Minds are necessary only to describe that phenomenon, not to make it true.

The fallacy of equivocation occurs because the TAG argument uses logical absolutes in more than one sense (3). Logical absolutes, as described in step one of the TAG argument above, are physical underpinnings of the universe; in step two, they are the descriptions of those laws, like the photograph described earlier. Logical absolutes do exist. However, these laws are not conceptual in nature. We do not need any minds for them to exit. We only need minds to observe, understand and express these laws. Furthermore, our perceptions of these laws are by no means perfect, unchanging or absolute.

Other Flaws with the Transcendental Argument

Even if the premises of TAG were sound, the argument still leaves much to be desired as evidence of the existence of God. If you were to accept the premise that universal concepts require a universal mind to think of them, there is nothing to suggest what that mind might be like.

In other words, the transcendent mind behind the rules of logic would not necessarily need to have any of the qualities commonly associated with deities, including benevolence, omnipotence, a role in the creation of the universe and a source of morality. There is nothing in the transcendental argument to suggest that the hypothetical mind behind the rules of logic was capable of or responsible for anything other than conceiving of those laws. As such, it would fail to actually prove anything about the existence of deities or provide convincing reason to worship or attempt to create personal relationships with god(s).

Sources:

1) Slick, Matt. "The Transcendental Argument for the Existence of God." CARM. Accessed September 16, 2014.

2) Kant, Immanuel and David Walford. "The Only Possible Argument in Support of a Demonstration of the Existence of God." *Theoretical Philosophy, 1755-1770*. Cambridge: Cambridge University Press, 1992.

3) Bennett, Bo. "Equivocation." *Logically Fallacious: The Ultimate Collection of over 300 Logical Fallacies*. EBookIt.com, 2012.

Chapter 15: "Believing in God provides meaning and purpose; without it, life would be meaningless."

Religion, particularly organized religion, provides many people with a sense of purpose and community. As we discussed in Chapter 12, religious communities can have many beneficial effects and often sit at the core of a person's cultural identity, but that does not make the claims of those religions true. In reality, religion itself does not assign meaning to an individual's life. Instead, individuals choose to give their lives meaning through the activities they pursue and the convictions they hold. Meaning can be found outside of religion, and seeking one's own meaning in life can be far more fulfilling than following the rules of an outside religious authority.

Religious Claims Are Not Proof

There's a common thread running throughout many of the claims in this book: believing in something does not make it true. Similarly, wanting something to be true does not affect its likelihood of actually being true. I might want to be a billionaire, but wanting it does not cause my bank account to swell. If I say that I'm a billionaire without anything to support that claim, no one has any reason to believe me. And if it turns out that I am not, in fact, a billionaire, then I am either a liar or delusional.

The same is true for religious beliefs. It doesn't matter whether believing in something makes you feel better about yourself or gives your life meaning; if there is no proof to substantiate those beliefs, they cannot act as evidence about the nature of reality.

When a person says, "Without God, life has no meaning," what he's really saying is: "I want to believe that life has meaning, and I can't imagine how that's possible without God, so I want to believe that God is real." While this desire is understandable, it's neither convincing nor necessary. It's possible to have a meaningful life without any religious convictions, and relying on religion to provide your life with significance can be psychologically damaging.

When you seek validation and meaning from outside sources, you risk being failed by the same institution that previously gave meaning to your life. Moreover, the culture of religion can lead to identical group thinking and loss of objectivity. When actions are informed by beliefs, false beliefs can give rise to dangerous or harmful actions.

An Uncomfortable Truth Is Always Better than a Comforting Lie

In order to indoctrinate their followers and secure obedience, religions frequently tear people down, creating an emptiness that must then be filled with Jesus, Allah or any other deity. People are told that they are inherently bad or sinful and that the only way to become good is by giving over control of their lives to faith. As there is no evidence that any of that is true, religion, in effect, is creating an imaginary problem simply so that it can sell an imaginary solution.

The learned helplessness created by religion can open the way for charlatans and con artists to take advantage of gullible, vulnerable people. False ideas about the universe, including promises that good people are rewarded and sinful people punished, can set false expectations among believers and strip them of the tools they need to properly cope with the challenging events of their lives in a healthy way.

It's often better to face reality head-on and attempt to cope with it directly rather than comfort oneself with deception. As Bertrand Russell once said, "No satisfaction based upon self-deception is solid, and, however unpleasant the truth may be, it is better to face it once for all, to get used to it, and to proceed to build your life in accordance with it."

We Are Free to Create Our Own Meaning

Part of the beauty and wonder of being alive is the opportunity to make your own choices and create your own meaning. Instead of having a predetermined "destiny" or some powerful guiding hand calling the shots in your life, you are free to seek your own meaning and value by making your own choices and discovering your own unique path.

There is no single outside force imposing meaning on the events of your life. There is no evidence whatsoever that people's life events conform to some sort of divine plan or predestination. Life is, objectively, meaningless; given the size and scope of the universe and our tiny role within it, it's absurd to think that we might have any sort of cosmically vital role.

The lack of external meaning to our lives can grant us a pleasant sense of freedom. Rather than being tethered by an outside force, we are free to explore the universe, seek answers to profound questions or enjoy simple pleasures, like sex and food. We have the ability to create meaning for our lives by setting worthwhile goals, working to improve the lives of those around us, enjoying our time on earth, making connections to other humans and loving our families. All of these activities are worthwhile, and none of them require the existence of God.

Chapter 16: "So many people died for God/religion. Surely, it must be real."

The study of world religions yields a bloody history. Holy wars have been fought between different factions of believers, martyrs have willingly given up their lives for their religious beliefs, people have been sacrificed to appease angry gods and victims have been tortured and killed in the name of religion.

This history says more about the violent and hurtful aspects of human nature than it does about the existence of God. The fact is that certain people are always willing to sacrifice themselves for something they believe in, regardless of whether those beliefs are religious in nature or not. Dying in the name of a religion is tragic and lamentable, but it does not prove that such actions are justified by the will of an existing deity.

People Will Die for What They Believe In

People have frequently been willing to risk their lives for political, religious or cultural reasons through actions like hunger strikes, self-immolation, violent protests and more. But logically, why would anyone choose to die or welcome death for reasons such as these? Many of these worldviews rely on belief systems that promote self-sacrifice as a method transcending death or a way to find greater purpose. These worldviews are sometimes religious, like the idea of an afterlife that renders mortal suffering irrelevant, or they may be secular, like the belief that one's actions can leave behind an immortal legacy by participating in a social cause. One theory offers an explanation for this common practice of assigning a greater meaning or notion of non-permanence to death: terror management theory (1). Essentially, the theory states that because humans are uniquely aware of their mortality, they create coping mechanisms to overcome the anxiety associated with it. Otherwise, people could live in constant, paralyzing fear of death. Therefore, humans create cultural worldviews that allow them to feel transcendent or believe that they are part of something immortal. The key in this instance of a person welcoming death for a particular cause is that the person feels as though he is part of something greater than himself and that his death will result in an eternity of immortal afterlife.

This might explain suicide cults, where otherwise rational people are willing to commit mass suicide. In 1997, 39 people in the Heaven's Gate community died believing that doing so would enable them to board a UFO that would save them from an imminent apocalypse (2). In the 1970s, Jim Jones pronounced himself a messiah and led more than 900 people to kill themselves (3). That so many people died through participation in these cults clearly does not mean that the claims of their founders were true. It could simply mean that these people were manipulated into feeling that they were part of something greater than themselves and that their deaths could be especially meaningful in the context of that belief system.

The Reality of Holy Wars

The tendency of humans to be attracted to martyrdom can be easily exploited, and this is clearly a factor in many of the religious conflicts throughout history. War is a complex issue, and wars are rarely ever fought for just one reason. Even so-called holy wars can have non-religious motivations, like revenge, politics or obtaining resources from neighboring communities. Yet religion plays a vital role in the recruitment and motivation process (4). It is far easier to recruit troops willing to die for a cause if that cause seems particularly transcendent. People might be unwilling to risk their lives for commercial success, but they might be more willing if they believe they are promoting an ideology or acting on a deity's will. It is also likely easier to convince someone to die for a cause if they believe that their earthly death is only the beginning of a blissful and eternal afterlife. After all, dying isn't such a big deal if you're not really dying.

In a conflict between two religions, at least one side would necessarily have to be wrong; they could not both be right, as each individual religious belief system is unique. Since fatalities exist on all sides of every conflict – there is no indication that a deity is overseeing these battles or choosing sides. People of many different religions have died for their religious beliefs. Martyrs come from Christianity, Islam, Hinduism and other religious backgrounds, and all of them believe that theirs is the right cause. They can't all be right. At least some martyrs must have died in vain. Mollified by a belief in an afterlife or some sort of cosmic reward, people are willing to waste or sacrifice their lives. With no evidence for an afterlife, we should recognize the true value of our current lives as our one and only shot at happiness. Wasting it on unfounded claims and ancient myths is an absolute tragedy.

Sources:

1) Routledge, Clay. "Understanding Self-Sacrifice: Suicide as Self-Transcendence." Psychology Today. January 19, 2011. Accessed September 21, 2014.

2) Zennie, Michael. "New Age Followers Still Waiting for Aliens to Beam Them up 15 Years after Heaven's Gate Cult Suicides Left 39 People Dead." Mail Online. March 26, 2012. Accessed September 21, 2014.

3) Hall, John R. "The Apocalypse at Jonestown (with Afterword)." *In gods we trust* (1981): 269.

4) "Suicide Terrorist Database - Flinders University- Australia." Terrorism Research & Analysis Consortium.

Chapter 17: "Atheism has killed more people than religion, so it must be wrong!"

Faced with the violence condoned and encouraged by organized religion, some believers are eager to point out that atheists are equally violent, if not more. In fact, some suggest that atheism is at the root of the worst atrocities in recent history, like the regime of Joseph Stalin or Mao Zedong. This idea goes hand in hand with the argument discussed in Chapter 4: that morality stems from God, so an atheistic government must be immoral.

While it's true that Stalin and Mao were corrupt leaders who denounced religion among their people, suggesting that their depravity was caused by atheism or that their behavior was at all indicative of atheism as a whole simply does not follow. Similarly, the idea that atheism is somehow uniquely responsible for despotism is clearly false. History is filled with examples of the religious whose beliefs were directly responsible for murder and violence (1). Yet such direct relationship has not been seen with secular tyrants. If anything, non-religious dictators themselves act more like religious zealots, elevating themselves as deities in the cult of personality they've developed.

Atheism Has No Doctrines

The violence within Christianity or Islam can often be traced back to the teachings of those religions because it is embedded in the ideology of the religions themselves (2). Even though war and violence in the name of God are often motivated by non-religious ambitions, such as political and territorial gain, religions in such cases are often used as an excuse for justifying such acts, disguising their intentions as holy and recruiting armies of people who would not have been willing to risk their lives for purely secular causes (3). People throughout history have been martyred and sacrificed in the name of religion, and holy wars have been fought over the tenets of those religions.

The same cannot be said of atheism for the simple fact that atheism is not a religion. Atheism is a lack of belief in deities. It has no governing dogmatic principles, no rule book and no core ideology. Comparing atheism to religion is like comparing apples and oranges. It's more helpful to compare atheism to theism, which is simply belief in a deity. While some theists also hold fundamentalist beliefs, just believing that some god exists is not enough to cause wars and violence based on the belief alone. How many wars have been caused by deism? You'd need some additional dogmatic beliefs in order for that happen.

No one commits mass murder in the name of theism or atheism alone. Additional dogmatic principles are needed to justify such grisly outcomes. In the case of theism, religions like Christianity and Islam provide such dogma, creating convenient excuses. Secular totalitarian regimes and religion share this dogmatic element: a belief that a set of ideas are true because an authority figure says so and that questioning those ideas can lead to serious or even deadly consequences.

Therefore, it's not reasonable to say that atheism condones or promotes violence or that tyrants have killed in the name of atheism. Such actions or any other action, both good and bad, do not and cannot speak for atheism in general, as no two atheists necessarily hold any of the same beliefs or convictions about the world. The only thing held in common between all atheists is a lack of belief in deities.

This means that some atheists are undoubtedly unkind, aggressive and violent. It also means that some atheists are kind, friendly and peaceful. Any type of person can be an atheist, just as any type of person can be not interested in golf. Just because some non-golfers are jerks doesn't make not golfing bad any more than atheism can be blamed for the behavior of a handful of atheists. If you're trying to make a decision about whether you believe in God based on how a certain non-believer you know acts, you're using flawed reasoning. For the same reason, not all religious people are bad or cruel individuals, yet the practice of violence and war is deeply imbedded in many religious ideologies. It is, therefore, best to examine your views about God or other religious beliefs by evaluating the evidence provided for such claims, not based on the behavior of people who do or do not accept it as truth.

The Cult of Personality

It's true that the tyrannical communist regimes of Mao and Stalin were opposed to religion, with religious belief discouraged and punished under their rule. This had less to do with atheism and more to do with the threat of religion as competition with their own tyrannical plans. Totalitarian regimes are built on dogma and fear, not freedom of speech and inquiry. In this way, they greatly resemble religion. In effect, these leaders essentially created religions and inserted themselves at the top as new deities. As Sam Harris put it, "The problem with fascism and communism, however, is not that they are too critical of religion; the problem is that they are too much like religions." These cults of personality are not derived from atheism, and it is hard to see how one could argue that their activities were representative of atheists as a whole. Indeed, many free, irreligious nations, such as Denmark and Sweden (4), are among the most peaceful and prosperous countries in the world (5). The point, however, is not to say that atheism necessarily causes people to be happier or more prosperous. What is clear, however, is that atheism does not lead to violence, tyranny or genocide any more than religiosity guarantees a peaceful and prosperous nation.

The world's religions have rules and holy books that tell their followers what's wrong or right and how to behave. Thus, it is reasonable to hold a religion accountable for the message that it preaches. There are no holy atheist scriptures, no atheist pope and no atheist rituals, tenets, creeds, code or authority. Atheism cannot be held accountable for the activities of atheists in the same way that religion can be judged by its doctrine because atheism has no doctrines.

Sources:

1) Hitchens, Christopher. *God is not great: How religion poisons everything*. Random House LLC, 2008.

2) Ellens, J. Harold. *The Destructive Power of Religion: Violence in Judaism, Christianity, and Islam*. Westport, Conn.: Praeger, 2003.

3) Juergensmeyer, Mark. *Terror in the Mind of God: The Global Rise of Religious Violence*. Vol. 13. Univ of California Press, 2003.

4) Zuckerman, Phil. "Atheism: Contemporary Numbers and Patterns." *In The Cambridge Companion to Atheism (Cambridge Companions to Philosophy)*. New York: Cambridge University Press, 2007.

5) *State of Global Well Being*. Gallup, 2013.

Chapter 18: "You'll become a believer when you are desperate for God's help."

According to the conventional wisdom of many believers, atheists frequently find themselves pulled toward God during times of stress, and they've come up with clever aphorisms to describe the phenomenon, like "there are no atheists in foxholes" or "only an atheist until the plane start to fall". The idea behind this is that it's easy to be an atheist when your life is going well, but once you experience hard times, you'll believe in God or at least hope that he is real.

While this claim may be true for some people, it's certainly not a universal truth among atheists. Moreover, the existence of "deathbed conversions" and similar experiences does not prove the existence of God. They only suggest that people are at their most irrational when frightened, in pain or delirious. The intense fear of death may drive some to accept illogical or irrational views out of desperation for comfort or a way to relieve or lessen their intense anxiety. We're all human and experience the same basic emotions, so this desire for comfort is certainly understandable. Then, it's not that someone is desperate for God; they're desperate for some kind of comfort and emotional relief.

The idea that fear could drive you toward the belief in God only goes to suggest that religious claims are commonly fear-based and not rooted in actual logic or evidence. Unintentionally, theists are essentially acknowledging that their claims are irrational.

Are There Really No Atheists in Foxholes?

Many atheists lost their faith in God through reasonable discourse and careful consideration. Such views are unlikely to change on a whim. An atheist suddenly believing in God is like a grown man suddenly believing in Santa Claus. For many atheists, the only thing that could genuinely cause them to change their minds is real evidence for God's existence, not the emotional turmoil of stress, death and tragedy.

Seven years after astronomer and science popularizer Carl Sagan died, his wife, Ann Druyan, said this about her husband:

> *"When my husband died, because he was so famous and known for not being a believer, many people would come up to me and ask me if Carl changed at the end and converted to a belief in an afterlife. They also frequently ask me if I think I will see him again. Carl faced his death with unflagging courage and never sought refuge in illusions. The tragedy was that we knew we would never see each other again. I don't ever expect to be reunited with Carl. But, the great thing is that when we were together, for nearly twenty years, we lived with a vivid appreciation of how brief and precious life is. We never trivialized the meaning of death by*

pretending it was anything other than a final parting. Every single moment that we were alive and we were together was miraculous-not miraculous in the sense of inexplicable or supernatural... The way he treated me and the way I treated him, the way we took care of each other and our family, while he lived. That is so much more important than the idea I will see him someday. I don't think I'll ever see Carl again. But I saw him. We saw each other. We found each other in the cosmos, and that was wonderful." (1)

Prior to his death, journalist and literary critic Christopher Hitchens stated in an interview with Anderson Cooper on CNN that if he had any deathbed conversion, it would be the product of delirium. He acknowledged that his brain may act erratically and outside of his control in his final hours but was confident that any actions it took would not represent who he really was:

Cooper: In a moment of doubt, isn't there?...I just find it fascinating that even when you're alone and no one else is watching, there might be a moment when you want to hedge your bets.

Hitchens: If that comes, it will be when I'm very ill, when I'm half demented either by drugs or by pain and I won't have control over what I say. I mention this in case you ever hear a rumor later on—because these things happen, and the faithful love to spread these rumors. Well, I can't say that the entity that by then wouldn't be me wouldn't do such a pathetic thing, but I can tell you that not while I'm lucid, no. I can be quite sure of that.

Cooper: So if there's some story that on your deathbed...

Hitchens: Don't believe it. Don't credit it. (2)

Evolutionary biologist and atheist activist Richard Dawkins said in an interview with Bill Maher:

"When I'm on my deathbed, I'm going to have a tape recorder switched on. Because people like me are the victims of malicious stories after their death, people saying they had a deathbed conversion when they didn't." (3)

A Dying Brain Cannot Be Trusted

Faced with extreme stress, pain, loss of blood, drugs and other similar factors, the brain sometimes acts differently than it normally would. Some patients come out of surgical anesthesia feeling extreme delirium, believing, for example, that their doctors are conspiring to kill them or simply seeing things that aren't there (4). That some of these hallucinations could be religious in nature is hardly surprising. Religious myths are widespread, and many people are exposed to religion from a young age. Such fables can easily resurface from the subconscious mind regardless of the person's conscious, rational beliefs.

Theists like to point to the global prevalence of religious belief as proof that there is a global desire to believe in God. The reality is more complex. Cultural indoctrination certainly plays a role. So does the nature of the human brain, which finds patterns in random noise and searches for explanations by assigning agency to events that are not caused by any agents (5). Humans have a lot of natural impulses and tendencies, but that doesn't mean we need to embrace them all. It should come as no surprise that human brains frequently act similarly. That we might have some desire to appeal to a higher deity says less about the reality of a god than it does about the way our brains are wired and our naturally human desire to understand the universe, regardless of whether such perceived understanding is based on verifiable evidence or ancient dogma.

Belief Does Not Influence Reality

As we've discussed time and again throughout this book, believing in something does not make it true. Just because someone may or may not change her mind about God does not make religious claims any more likely. Insisting that an atheist will convert on her deathbed or stating that a person's views will crumble in times of crisis is both patronizing and irrelevant.

There is no shame in strange deathbed experiences or temporary reversions in times of crisis. People do not have any control over what their brains do when under a state of duress, and it's hardly representative of their views if they do or say strange things when faced with death, illness or tragedy. Using the behavior of a person made vulnerable by tragedy as an excuse to promote a religious agenda is utterly reprehensible.

Sources:

1) Druyan, Ann. "Ann Druyan Talks About Science, Religion, Wonder, Awe... and Carl Sagan." *Skeptical Inquirer* 27, no. 6 (2003): 25-30.

2) Christopher Hitchens. "Author Hitchens Talks Cancer and God." CNN. August 5, 2010. Accessed September 25, 2014.

3) Richard Dawkins. "Real Time with Bill Maher." New York, NY: HBO. April 11, 2008.

4) Dobson, Roger. "How Having an Operation Can Send You Delirious: Terrifying Post-surgery Hallucinations Strike up to Half of the Over-65s." Mail Online. September 10, 2012. Accessed September 25, 2014.

5) Shermer, Michael. *The Believing Brain: From Ghosts and Gods to Politics and Conspiracies – How We Construct Beliefs and Reinforce Them as Truths*. St. Martin's Griffin, 2012.

Chapter 19: "Smart people and renowned scientists like X, Y and Z believe in God, so it must be true."

Some theists will use this line of defense when questioned about their beliefs: "Person X is very intelligent, and he believes in God. Who am I to say he's wrong?" It's a natural inclination for people to accept the views of people in authority. From a young age, we are conditioned to respond to authority. We learn that our parents know better than we do and that we should do what they say. When we enter school, we learn to listen to our teachers. Our society functions in large part because we rely on people in authority to be knowledgeable (1).

To an extent, this reliance on authority is necessary. After all, teachers and parents generally do know better than the children in their care. Law and order can only be maintained if citizens respect the authority of the police. However, the natural tendency to believe what we're told can lead to intellectual laziness, with people not bothering to think critically about their lives and examine whether claims and ideas are actually true.

Experts are not always right. Even very smart people can be wrong. Likewise, smart people can be wrong about God. A person's intelligence does not cause her to be right; an intelligent person who fails to recognize material evidence can still hold the wrong opinion.

Smart People Can Be Wrong

It's a mistake to confuse intelligence with knowledge. Intelligence relates to the way one processes information, not necessarily what she knows or believes. This can lead to an individual making complex justifications to defend her beliefs, even when those beliefs are clearly false. For example, Sir Arthur Conan Doyle, physician and the author of the famous Sherlock Holmes stories, believed in fairies (1). As science historian Michael Shermer notes, "Smart people believe weird things because they are better at rationalizing their beliefs that they hold for non-smart reasons."

The Appeal to Authority

An appeal to authority is a logical fallacy that usually takes the following form:

Person A is an expert in Z.
Person A said X about Z.
Therefore, X must be true.

This is a fallacy because person A's opinion or misinformed conclusion does not actually affect the truth, and experts are not always right (2). An expert's opinion or interpretation is frequently closer to the truth than other people's opinions, because she is well educated on a topic. That view, however, is not automatically correct simply because one is an expert about something, and being an expert does not make one's opinions or conclusions automatically more valid. Experts can and often do make mistakes.

Simply stated, a fact isn't true because someone said it was. Valid scientific findings are accepted as most likely true because they can be independently tested and validated. Scientific authority stretches only so far as the scientist's ability to accurately report on the results of such testing. Therefore, accepting a claim only because an expert made it and ignoring evidence to support or refute the claim flies in the face of the scientific method.

Pointing out this logical fallacy should not be used to dismiss expert opinions or conclusions out of hand. It should, however, be kept in mind any time a claim's veracity rests solely on the authority of the person making it. If an expert has no evidence to support her claim or if her claim cannot be reproduced and tested, her view is hardly more reliable than that of anybody else.

Atheism, Education and Intelligence

Belief is not merely a matter of intelligence. It's an issue of what information a person has available and how she processes that information. Atheism often comes down to asking the right questions or spotting the problems in belief; a person who has not been exposed to those doubts or who has never had an occasion to question those beliefs might never consider atheism, regardless of her intelligence. Similarly, belief in a deity does not automatically make someone stupid.

To be sure, a number of highly intelligent people throughout history have believed in God. Yet some data seem to suggest a strong positive correlation between intelligence and atheism (3). The reasons for this are complex and tied in part to the socioeconomic trends and not necessarily a direct cause of higher intelligence. Nevertheless, it's not difficult to imagine that many atheists arrived at their position through skepticism and critical thought, skills which do require some level of intelligence. Critically examining the claims of religions allows a person to see through them, recognizing the fallacies they contain. This might be why atheism is much more common among scientists as among non-scientists (4). Such data do not support or negate the existence of a deity. Yet they do refute arguments claiming the prevalence of theistic views among intellectuals as a way of supporting a belief in God.

Ultimately, the level of intelligence shown by believers and non-believers has little to do with the reality of God's existence. If it did, then the existence of intelligent atheists would be equally as compelling as the claims of intelligent theists. Both views cannot be right. Without evidence, there is no reason to believe the claims of any individual, regardless of their expertise, intelligence or level of education.

Sources:

1) Cialdini, Robert B. "Authority." *Influence: The Psychology of Persuasion*. Rev. Ed. ; 1st ed. New York: Harper Business, 2006.2) Moosa, Tauriq. "The Dangers of Being Smart." Big Think. June 13, 2012. Accessed September 26, 2014.

Chapter 20: "How can we really know *anything?*"

Extreme skepticism is a form of philosophical skepticism that considers it impossible to believe anything (1). Where atheists claim that we have not proved that God exists, an extreme skeptic would say, "We cannot prove that anything exists." Some would take this to imply that God's existence and non-existence are equally likely.

At its mildest, extreme skepticism raises the question of whether any particular view can be proven or considered objectively correct. In its strongest form, such skepticism can lead to a total rejection of the physical world. As a philosophical quandary, skepticism of this kind has existed for thousands of years (1).

How Can We Know Anything?

Before showing why this argument cannot be used to counter atheism, it helps to understand exactly what is meant by skepticism in this sense. The reason that some claim that true knowledge is impossible is because we are limited by our senses and experiences, which are ultimately subjective. We perceive reality through our senses and think about it with our brains, and it's impossible to know for sure whether these senses are actually trustworthy.

For example, consider the color blue. We understand scientifically that the color is caused by a specific wavelength of light bouncing off of an object, and we can measure the length of waves to determine whether a color can be classified as blue. We cannot, however, say with absolute certainty that the color we perceive as blue actually looks the same to anyone else. Because we cannot see through other people's eyes, we can't know for sure how colors look to them.

Indeed, it's possible that we do not even really exist and that there is no such thing as reality. We could all be brains in vats, hooked up to a computer simulation, like in the famous movie *The Matrix*; everything you know and experience may be a lie. As the logic of this argument goes, we have no way of knowing whether we're actually brains in vats; therefore, we have no way of knowing anything else about our world. Since this claim is in no way testable, however, we have no way of proving it and no reason to believe that it's true. We can only live in the reality we can observe, not a hypothetical reality that we have no way of proving. To do otherwise would be insane.

For example, imagine that someone tells you that there is a monster living beneath your bed. You can never know that he's there, however, because he is invisible, makes no noise and leaves no trace of his existence. Since there is no way of proving that such a monster exists and since its existence is very unlikely given that it contradicts many highly predictive scientific models explaining our universe, there is simply no reason to act as though there's a monster under your bed. Since such an unfalsifiable monster is indistinguishable from a monster that doesn't exist, it is most practical to simply live as though there is no monster.

Are you currently awake, or is this a dream? Maybe you are still in bed. Maybe when you wake up, you'll remember that you are not even who you think you are at this moment in your dream. You might have a different name, gender or race. You might not even be human. Or you might be just a character in someone else's dream or an advanced computer game. And once whoever is dreaming this dream wakes up or turns off the gaming console, you would cease to exist. You can't prove any of this is not true, but would it be reasonable to make any decisions based on these or the unlimited number of other unfalsifiable claims?

We do not require absolute certainty about our world. We can act on the information available to us, making the best choice possible with what we can know with some but not an absolute level of certainty. Such levels of certainty are sufficient for us to act upon. Science doesn't claim to have absolute certainty about the world; it creates models that provide the best explanation based on the available evidence. If additional evidence is found, the model can be changed. Religious claims should stand up to the same scrutiny as scientific ones; claims should be testable, repeatable and falsifiable. If there is no way to test whether a claim is true, there is no reason to live as though it is.

Beliefs Can Be Justified

We have no choice but to live in reality and obey the laws that govern it as they are perceived. Even if our reality were only a simulation, it's the only option available to us, and so we base our beliefs about the world on what we can observe. We don't wait until we have absolute certainty before acting; we make decisions about our world based upon what our experiences can tell us of the laws of our universe.

Carl Sagan once said, "Extraordinary claims require extraordinary evidence." If you make a claim that does not contradict our current understanding of the universe, some basic level of data would be sufficient to support it. For example, if you claim that the sun will rise around 6 a.m. tomorrow, I could be inclined to believe you. Depending on the time of year and geographical location, I could determine whether your claim is consistent with what I could expect. If, however, you tell me that the sun will not rise tomorrow and will instead be eaten by a giant wolf in the sky, I'll need significantly more evidence. Everything I can observe about reality suggests that this is incredibly unlikely, as it disregards many apparent laws of the universe. Before I could accept such an extraordinary claim, I would need some very compelling evidence. Otherwise, it would be much more likely to assume that you were insane or simply lying.

Saying that we can't really know whether God exists does nothing to prove that it does. Not being able to know something for certain does not increase the odds of it being true. Unlike extreme forms of skepticism, scientific skepticism evaluates the likelihood of a claim by the strength of the evidence supporting it. Using such methods, we can assess the likelihood of claims. Unfalsifiable claims, such as God, Santa Claus or leprechauns, are not as likely as claims with strong testable, verifiable and repeatable evidence (2). Time and again, the scientific method has, more consistently than any other method, been successful at providing explanations with very accurate predictive power for our universe. This can easily be seen in the success of technological advancements in the past century and has justified belief in the stability of natural laws.

I Reject Your Reality and Substitute My Own

On the TV show *Mythbusters,* Adam Savage famously quipped, "I reject your reality and substitute my own" (3). He was joking, but the sentiment is one that can be easily applied to people who subscribe to the sort of extreme skepticism described throughout this chapter: if we cannot truly know anything, then anything could be true.

While there may be merit in discussing such ideas from a philosophical standpoint, it doesn't hold water as an argument for the existence of God. If we accept this argument as true, then we also cannot be certain that this argument is correct, as certainty would refute the very basis of the argument.

All of this philosophizing is really just a distraction from the fact that theists cannot prove the existence of their god. It is not the burden of atheists to defend their lack of belief, and atheists do not need to have all of the answers about the world in order to lack belief in a deity. Theists, by claiming that God exists, are making an extraordinary claim. This requires extraordinary evidence. As seen throughout this book, that evidence does not exist. No argument laid out by theists so far is compellingly believable.

Sources:

1) Dancy, Jonathan, Ernest Sosa, and Matthias Steup, eds. *A Companion to* Epistemology. 2nd ed. Wiley-Blackwell, 2010.

2) Kurtz, Paul. The New Skepticism. Prometheus Books, 1992.

3) Savage, Adam. "Explosive Decompression/Frog Giggin'/Rear Axle." MythBusters. Discovery Channel. 11 Jan. 2004.

In Pursuit of God

Why There Is No God was written by Armin Navabi. A former Muslim, Armin is the founder of Atheist Republic, a growing community with more than one million followers worldwide where atheists can share their views and engage in debates and discussion with other atheists and also believers. As a Muslim and later as an atheist, Armin found contemplating the idea of God and the effects of this concept to be an integral part of his life. His struggle to find God and a path into his grace almost cost him his life. The following segment is Armin's story as described by his friend and fellow member of the Atheist Republic team, Mohammad Savage.

An Opening Mind

Armin was born and raised in the Islamic Republic of Iran. He was indoctrinated quite thoroughly since early childhood in the Muslim tradition. He would pray regularly five times a day, as all Muslims are mandated to. Growing up, he was afraid of all the things which good Muslims are supposed to be afraid of: hell, sin, the devil, etc. The only thing which terrified him more than the thought of his own everlasting torment was the possibility of his parents being sent to hell. To his young mind, this was a very real possibility since they didn't pray regularly five times a day, as he did.

During his formative years, Armin attended Muslim classes. In such classes, he learned that according to his Islamic teachers, if a boy were to perish prior to the age of 15, access to heaven would be guaranteed, regardless of any other extenuating circumstances. The same rule also applied to girls; however, for them, the cutoff age is 9. This thought stuck with Armin, and driven by the fear instilled in him by his religion, it began to consume him.

In his young mind, there it was: a surefire, absolute method to gain access to that which many Muslims strive for their entire lives. It confounded him to no end that none of his peers or elders had discovered or taken advantage of such a wonderful and easy shortcut. He would not be one such sheep; he wouldn't allow the joys of a full life to pull the wool over his young eyes. His future course of action became crystal clear. At age 14, after making up his mind and stealing his resolve, Armin launched himself from one of the higher windows in his school.

This was his attempt to end his life and guarantee his future ascendance. Needless to say, it didn't work out quite as he had hoped. Armin survived his suicide attempt but was ravaged by injury. Among the injuries he suffered were a broken wrist, two broken legs and an injured back. After the accident, Armin was confined to a wheelchair for the next seven months. Even after regaining permission to ambulate further, he still required months before he was able to travel with some semblance of independence.

Wracked by more than the physical injuries of his failed suicide attempt, Armin was torn apart by the effect his actions had on his parents. Seeing the impact it had on them, Armin was no longer deluded by the temptation of an easy way to heaven, and so, he dedicated himself even more so to his religion and finding a better path to God. He prayed more frequently, studied Islam in detail, attempted to learn all he could to be a better Muslim and regularly begged his parents to follow suit. Not a day passed that he wouldn't request his mother to join him in his daily prayers.

While his newfound dedication and studies did lead him to become more familiar with the intricacies of his religion, it also led to some rather unexpected and quite unwelcome thoughts. For every question his studies answered about his religious beliefs and the nature of God, ten more popped up in their stead, leading to a seemingly endless and inconclusive search. The more he studied, the more questions he had and the more confused he became. He started to question God as well as God's motives, and judgments. For example, why would a benevolent God send people to hell simply because they picked the wrong religion?

Such novel questions did not come without a price. Every time Armin found himself questioning God, he felt the cold, creeping fingers of guilt grip his heart. Led by his thirst for knowledge and knowing that seeking Islamic knowledge is encouraged in his religion, he convinced himself that studying the nature of his God could never be a reprehensible act. Emboldened by his newfound sense of purpose, he set out to study and learn all he could about more religions, including some dead religions. He was fueled with curiosity for why, according to Islam, these religions were so evil that all of their followers were damned to eternal hellfire and brimstone. What did they get wrong? What were their major errors? The more he studied, the more he learned and the more and more he began to see the fallacies of all of these other religions, including his own. Through countless hours spent studying, researching and pondering, he began to see the greater possibility that religion could indeed have been a manmade concept.

Having been trained to fear all of the thoughts he had swimming in his head, Armin found himself tortured. His sleep was punctured by nightmares of the gates of hell opening for him. His days were drowned in visions of devils and demons out to punish him, making him pay for his insolence. As a practicing Muslim, he was aware that what he was thinking was not only wrong, but downright evil. He was aware that God could see into his thoughts. He could feel the disappointment God felt in him. He was depressed by the knowledge that he had let his best friend, his protector and creator, down. However, no matter how horrid he felt, once the doubts about religion began to appear, they stuck. The lingering doubts regarding his creator blossomed; they inspired further research and contemplation.

The more he began to think of religion as a manmade concept, not a divine statute, the stronger his doubt became. No longer able to abide the growing storm inside of him, Armin resolved to face the matter directly, disregard his doubts and attempt to convince himself simply that God was real and that he could be absolutely certain of this. He simply needed proof, actual, verifiable proof, not the mythos of a centuries-old novel. He believed once he managed to locate this proof, his faith would be stronger than ever.

Failing to find proof, he settled on any logical reasoning for the existence of God, including examining philosophical concepts and theories. However, once all of the logical explanations supporting God had been thoroughly debunked, he grew desperate. He prayed harder, begging God to help him. He wanted a sign, a message – anything at all to assure himself of a divine presence. Of course, his prayers were never answered. All of this transpired during most of Armin's relatively young life, and by the age of 18, he had lost all of his faith. He felt cheated, betrayed and taken advantage of by society, his country, teachers, and those who impose the belief in God as an absolute truth without any proof, denying all other alternatives. He felt angry, depressed, and broken. He had sacrificed so much, even almost his life, all for the sake of a fairytale.

Of course, as it sometimes happens when leaving a lifelong religion, Armin had moments of doubt. "Perhaps I'm mistaken. Perhaps there's something really wrong with me. Perhaps my fall broke more than my bones; perhaps it broke my mind. Am I really so arrogant to think that I've managed to discover something that no one else around me has realized?" These were all common topics for self-debate during this period of self-discovery. Armin was the only atheist he knew. Being the proactive go-getter he had always been, he wished to let more people know about his lack of belief as well as the amazing journey which had led to this conclusion.

Life in an Islamic state was becoming exceedingly lonely for a newly formed atheist. He yearned to share his experiences and thoughts and took to Orkut (a pre-Facebook social networking site) to create what would become the spiritual predecessor to the Atheist Republic. Beyond his initial fears, he was shocked and pleasantly surprised to see so many people join his community and discuss the topic at hand. He was elated to find others like himself. The crazy notion of a nonexistent God certainly didn't seem so crazy anymore.

Armin wished to reach more people and touch a larger audience. He simply wanted to find more atheists and discuss God and religion with any interested parties, but above all, he wished for people to be made aware that atheism was a legitimate option. It was one of his life's greatest examples of unfairness that he wasn't given a chance to choose.

Unsatisfied with the current reach and exposure, he started the Atheist Republic in 2011. The main purpose of this community was to let everyone know about the many people who didn't believe in God and provide an invitation for them to explore these ideas if they were interested. He also wanted to create a community for atheists. He wanted them to feel less lonely and ashamed. He wanted them to know that not only are there others like us, but that there are people out there willing to listen, support and guide them.

Further Debates and Discussions

The focus of this book is on the concept of God, not specific religions. In my two upcoming books, I will discuss the specifics of Islam and Christianity and reveal the main problems with the teachings of these two world religions. If you leave an honest review for *Why There Is No God* on Amazon or Goodreads, we'll send you a pre-released copy of either of these books absolutely free as soon as they become available. Simply send us a link to the review by visiting AtheistBookReview.com, and we'll send you a free copy of either book as soon as it's ready. Your reviews will help us reach out to more people who might benefit from this text and future material.

While this book was meant to be concise, there is much more that can be said about the topics included in each chapter. If you'd like to further discuss any topic with me directly, you can schedule an online video or audio discussion with me at WhyThereIsNoGod.com. While you're there, I also invite you to sign up for the Atheist Republic newsletter for unique insights and stories from the Atheist Republic community. For feedback, suggestions or any other inquiries, feel free to contact me at ArminNavabi.com.

Armin kissing the Quran on the first day of the school year at age 11 or 12.

Made in the USA
San Bernardino, CA
13 July 2015